Eddy Brimson was born in 1964, the youngest of six children. Raised in Hemel Hempstead, Eddy left school with few qualifications but went on to set up a successful graphic design business before turning to writing in 1995.

Over the years Eddy has appeared on television and radio in many different guises, from presenter through to chat show guest and even *EastEnders* villain. In May '99 he set out on his latest passion, stand-up comedy and in December 2000 launched the website *footballtribe.com*, where he can be contacted via the following e-mail address: eddy@footballtribe.com

God Save
The Team

Fighting For Survival
at Euro 2000

Eddy Brimson

HEADLINE

First published in 2001
by HEADLINE BOOK PUBLISHING

10 9 8 7 6 5 4 3 2 1

ISBN 0 7472 3322 5

Typeset by Avon Dataset Ltd, Bidford-on-Avon, Warks

Printed and bound in Great Britain by
Mackays of Chatham plc, Chatham, Kent

HEADLINE BOOK PUBLISHING
A division of Hodder Headline
338 Euston Road
London NW1 3BH

www.headline.co.uk
www.hodderheadline.com

Contents

Dedication

This book is for Harriet, the world's top wife, and Arthur, a top cat. Thanks for all your love, support and attention. Big Love XXXX

Big Thanks also to all those I met along the way, even the Scummers! Take care and never let the bastards steal what is rightly ours.

Oh and Keef . . . Was that fun or what! A sexshe time, yesh!

Eddy.

PART ONE
The Build-up

1

Pack Up Your Troubles

I'll start this book with a joke:

Davo decides to sell up, leave the rat race and move to Greece. Once settled in, he goes about the business of meeting the locals and finding out who's who; then one day while walking in the hills he comes across a man herding goats. Eager to make acquaintances, he introduces himself. 'Hello, friend, my name is Davo.' The pair shake hands and then Davo continues the conversation: 'And what, may I ask, do they call you, sir?'

Suddenly the Greek becomes very embarrassed and his gaze diverts to the floor. 'Sir, many years ago there was a fire at the village school. Many of the children were trapped inside the building, screaming and crying. It was terrible. Without any thought for my own safety I beat back the flames and one by one pulled the children free.'

Davo is amazed by the shepherd's story. 'Sir, that is quite incredible!'

'Thank you, kind sir,' replies the shepherd. 'But, sir, do they call me "Stavros, the hero of our children"? No.' The man looks down and shakes his head. He then points to a chapel sitting high up on the hillside opposite. 'Sir, you see the chapel? Many years ago the nuns of the village were suddenly removed from the old chapel we once had in the village. They had occupied it for centuries but evil men came, men who wanted to reclaim the land and build the new motorway – the motorway you see over there runs right where their place of worship once stood. The nuns were destitute, they had nowhere to go, and so with my own bare hands I spent every spare minute, day and night, building a new chapel for them: the chapel you now see on the hill over there. But do they call me "Stavros, the builder of the chapel"? No.' Then the man suddenly becomes angry and begins to wave his fist in the direction of the village before announcing, 'But I shag just one goat . . .'

I use this joke as an analogy. Just like Stavros the shepherd, I too once dropped what is commonly known as a 'major-league bollock' and it is something I can't shake off to this day.

Within the pages of my first book I stuck my head above the trench, held my hands up and openly admitted that during a short period of my life, from my late teens to mid-twenties, I had been involved in football violence. The confession appeared in *Everywhere We Go*, which I co-wrote and which was first published in 1996. It was a confession made for many different reasons but with hindsight was one of the biggest mistakes I could ever have made.

I say that because it seems we live in a society where certain folk can kick the living daylights out of their girlfriend in a bar and yet all is forgiven once the ball starts hitting the back of the net or the next million-pound transfer comes along. Others preach to kids the evils of drugs then scuttle off to the toilet and whack a line of coke up their nose, following which there's the obligatory stay at the Priory from where they resurface, write a song and suddenly become seen as *oh so rock 'n' roll*. Hundreds of people daily log on to the likes of shaven-asian-lesbian-bondage-puppy-dogs-on-ice.com, download the pictures and send them to all and sundry because . . . well, it's all just a bit of a laugh, really. It's seen as life, accepted. It's not that nice but hey, shit happens. Confess that you were once a football hooligan, however, and boy, are you stuffed. Like herpes, the tag 'football hooligan' sticks with you forever, no matter how many years pass, no matter how many apologies you make. Once a football hooligan, always a football hooligan, the leper of modern European culture. And like an idiot I shot myself right in the foot. Indeed, I could have murdered my wife and buried her in a shallow grave, and if I'd have been caught I would have done my time and been released by now. On my release I'd have probably been given a flat, a job and a grant to go and have a nice holiday somewhere, just get my head together. But chase or – more likely in my case – get chased up a few side-roads on a Saturday afternoon and, just like Stavros, you're an outcast. Don't get me wrong, in no way am I trying to excuse my actions. I turned into a right little shit every Saturday, but like a lot of blokes my age who were involved back then I have, believe it or not, grown up, settled down and moved on in life.

The fact that my involvement in football hooliganism stopped long before the start of the European Championship finals in Germany 1988 – more than twelve years ago, I might add – cuts no ice. The fact that I have no criminal convictions means nothing to those who see no further than a shock-headline or a punchy radio interview. And the notion that the book was offered as a warning about what was slowly but surely coming back to haunt the game went unheeded, as at the time did the numerous solutions suggested within its pages towards combating the problem. It is funny to see that many of those solutions have since been put in motion and finally given the freedom to prove their effectiveness, but I very much doubt that any thanks will ever come my way. Perhaps those constructive solutions in fact added to my problems. After all, here was the so called 'enemy' telling the trusted authorities how to sort things out, and we can't have that, can we?

I made my confession in the naïve belief that adding some kind of honesty to the issues raised in my book would be appreciated. Honesty was clearly needed at the time, when far too many academics were creating jobs for themselves and spouting off about a subject of which they clearly lacked true understanding. Rather than hiding behind the notion that I was some kind of spectator, a voyeur who just somehow *knew* what drew young men into the movement, I put myself up as someone who had seen what goes on, from the inside. I had hoped to provide an insight into how the movement worked, knowledge that I felt could prove useful if taken on board and acted upon correctly. I have always believed that in order to sort out a problem you need to understand its root causes, otherwise you just waste a hell of a lot of time pissing in the wind. I never once pretended to be a major player, a member of a top hardcore firm or even some kind of hard-man. I was just a young lad who, like thousands of other young lads at that time, got caught up in a movement that was our version of the mods and rockers of the sixties – and believe me, back in the seventies and eighties there *were* thousands involved week in, week out across the country. The majority of the tales and personal accounts posted in *Everywhere We Go* and the other books I have written belong to other people and are not my own experiences. This is something that was always clearly stated but which often went unnoticed, even by those who went on to write books on the subject themselves.

In 1995, when I first started writing, football was undergoing the greatest transformation it had ever seen, and with Euro 96 on the horizon the game had reached an all-time high in the popularity stakes. Money was the new god, the answer to all footballs evils. Clubs were busy building shiny new stadiums, stadiums that were safer but somehow lacking atmosphere and kind of plastic. The game was attracting new fans whom some would argue mirrored their new surroundings. Football was more than happy with its new-found status, and quite rightly so – after so long in the doldrums it had every reason to be. The FA, didn't need any reminders of the darker side of the game. They didn't want any mention of the bad old days, days when the hooligans ruled the terraces and dragged the game into the gutter. Football had come up smelling of roses and in no way did they want to have their noses rubbed back in the dirt.

During the build-up to Euro 96 the game had convinced itself and the public that the football hooligan was and would remain a thing of the past, when in truth the violence had merely shifted to other arenas: the side-streets, pubs and train stations that linked our football stadiums. The FA successfully fooled the world into believing that Euro '96 was trouble free, something they continue to do even to this day. Yet despite the numerous warnings that have occurred in and around our football stadiums since the violence witnessed in Trafalgar Square in the summer of '96, it would appear that for fear of seeing what just might lurk in the shadows no one took a precautionary look over their shoulder.

I began writing because unlike those who ruled the game I refused to stick my head in the sand prior to the 1996 tournament, though for not one moment did I actually expect to see my words put into print. It gives me no pleasure to utter the patronising words 'I told you so', but I could see back then that, like me, the FA were on the verge of dropping a major-league bollock: the mistake of believing their own propaganda and the misconception that football violence was well and truly under control. My first book shocked a lot of people. Joe Public became aware of the fact that rather than being sporadic outbursts of hooliganism involving skinheads, losers and lager louts, football violence was in fact more often than not organised and premeditated. Here was a movement involving people from all walks of life. Suddenly the public began to realise that many of the hooligans they were seeing on their TV screens were more than likely people holding down respectable jobs, such as shop owners, financial advisers and possibly even your next-door neighbour's husband, rather than the stereotypes that the British media so stupidly portray even to this day. During the past five years much has happened in and around the football stadiums of England. The warning signs throughout mainland Europe have been there for all to see. The beach- and street-battles that took place in the city of Marseille during the World Cup finals of France 98 delivered the starkest reminder of what can go wrong when different countries and cultures meet in the name of football, and still the problem was left to fester until, like a spot on the chin of some pizza-faced teenager, it popped when we least wanted it to.

Then came the wake-up call, the season 1999–2000. The sandpit can no longer provide a hiding place for those who run the game both in this country and throughout Europe. The notion that hooliganism occurs only where stadiums are in need of upgrading has proved to be the lie many always knew it to be, a fact clearly illustrated on these shores following major incidents at Millwall, Stoke and Wigan. All these clubs have invested millions in new stadiums following the recommendations of the Taylor Report into ground safety, and yet the violence persisted. Fighting in Glasgow between rival Scottish and English fans; the tragic death of a Swansea City supporter at Rotherham; the list goes on and on. But there's the feeling that events outside the top flight somehow don't count, that they are easy to brush aside. Nevertheless, as the English Football Association desperately try to divert attention away from violence involving the clubs at the top end of the sport, they can't disguise the fact that once again every club within the Premiership was forced to report incidents of hooliganism in or around their stadium.

As some kind of cheap excuse for their own failure to deal with the problem here, the FA have constantly diverted people's gaze towards mainland Europe, citing there as the new home of the football hooligan. They have been quick in pointing an accusing finger in the directions of Germany, Belgium, Hungary and Poland. I don't for one minute deny that the so-called 'English disease' has in those countries caught up and indeed overtaken our own domestic problems, but unfortunately all this appears to have done is offer our own Football Association an air of complacency. In reality, violence elsewhere provided nothing more than a smoke-screen – a smoke-screen blown away by the violence which surrounded the UEFA Cup games in both Istanbul and Copenhagen and which involved supporters of Leeds United, Arsenal and the Turkish side Galatasaray. There can be no doubt that the incidents witnessed on the streets of the Danish capital were fuelled by the cold-blooded murders of the Leeds United supporters Kevin Speight and Christopher Loftus on the streets of Istanbul on 5 April 2000. While the TV images of the violence resulting in the deaths of those two innocent fans sickened the vast majority of right-minded people within our society, to others they sent an additional message. Rather than saying: 'Look, this has to stop, people are actually getting killed, for god's sake!' and rather than demonstrating that loss of life because of something so futile as football is a total, tragic waste, those images marked the throwing down of a gauntlet. A gauntlet just waiting to be picked up and slapped around some other poor innocent person's face.

I watched the coverage of Istanbul alone in a hotel room in Plymouth. It reminded me of what I had witnessed in Marseille, of the guy I saw on the beach who had just been stabbed and of how close I had come to taking a beating while working my way through the side-streets back to my hotel. These were images and memories that sent a shiver down my spine and had me wondering why I should even bother placing myself in such a situation again. A month or so later I watched the footage from Copenhagen on the lunchtime news while my wife sat next to me. The look on her face said it all – her horror, her disbelief and her contempt for those involved. To her, it all appeared pathetic beyond reason, beyond any explanation, and of course she was totally correct. And yet anyone with an ounce of common knowledge could have seen that Copenhagen was a riot just waiting to happen; and once again, happen it did.

As I sat with my wife watching the violence, I felt both ashamed and embarrassed to think that I had once been part of this horror. I felt ashamed of myself and embarrassed for my wife. I also began to wonder whether those that rule over the game felt the same emotions. I felt ashamed of the violence and embarrassed that little has been done to stop it. As the years roll by and the money stacks up, the mistakes remain the same, as do many of the people who sit at the head of football's governing bodies, those ultimately responsible for sorting the problem out. However, you can be sure that unlike me they will never hold up their hands, admit their sorry history and own up to their failings. As Euro 2000 drew nearer it became apparent that if the game was to continue to prosper the most important results would come not on the playing fields of Belgium and Holland but in the public squares, the back-streets and the travel terminals. And it was with that in mind that I found myself having to make a new confession as I packed my bag and changed my currency.

This book is about the high and lows of being an English football fan on foreign soil. It tells of my personal experiences when mixing with the English fans, and centres not just on the football but also the experiences such trips provide. Euro 2000 offered me more than I could have ever expected, but prior to heading off to the Low Countries my body and mind were racing with a variety of emotions and feelings. I was excited at the prospect of seeing some outstanding football; I was buzzing at the thought of travelling to new cities and visiting new stadiums; and once again I was optimistic about meeting new people, the weird, the wonderful and even the wankers. I held in my mind the dream of all dreams – that of actually being present when England won their first trophy for thirty-four years. But above all else, and here is that confession, folks: the thought of going to Euro 2000 actually scared me shitless.

2

When You Finally Realise
it is Only a Game After All!

The night of Wednesday 5 April 2000 must remain for ever etched in the minds of English football supporters the world over, for it marks the murders of two Leeds United fans, Christopher Loftus and Kevin Speight, on the streets of Istanbul, the pair of them having fallen victim to a rampaging mob of murdering Galatasaray football hooligans.

Their murders stunned this nation and above all left the families, friends and relatives of those involved with a void in their lives which shall forever remain. It is with this in mind that I ask you to do what the FA deemed unnecessary: please just take a minute and sit in silence as a mark of respect before reading any further.

Thank you.

There can be no doubt that a trip to watch football in Turkey is seen by some as a challenge. It's that *something* many football supporters have tucked away in the back of their brain. The dicing with danger, the thrill of the moment and the desire to come back to your mates and say you've been there, done it. Galatasaray are a team with a reputation, a violent history and a 'Welcome to hell' motto which fuels that desire more than almost any other club in the world. Thus some would argue that the events of that fateful night should not have been unpredictable.

During the afternoon and into the early evening of that day, the Leeds fans had mixed happily with the locals, enjoying the banter while singing their songs. As their numbers grew, however, so too did a large group of Galatasaray fans outside the Borsa restaurant just off the main square. The night wore on, the drink flowed and both groups grew more boisterous. Then, at approximately 8.45 p.m., all hell broke loose. Just what sparked the trouble is hard to establish; the Turks offered up a whole host of excuses while many English claimed a totally unprovoked attack. Suggestions that some Leeds fans had been openly urinating in the streets and behaving like animals were commonplace among the Turks. The alleged abuse of a passing workman was yet another claim thrown in, as was the accusation levelled against the Leeds fans drinking in the Aspen bar who, according to one Turkish eyewitness, had taken down the Turkish flag from the wall and used it to imitate whipping their backsides. Though whatever it was that lit the blue touch-paper will perhaps remain clouded, the next few hours were to provide images that persist in the memories of many fans, as they led to the murder of two innocent football fans.

Many of those present shared the belief that the violence orchestrated against the Leeds fans that night had been organised well in advance. People pointed out the fact that many of the Turkish hooligans involved had come prepared, carrying weapons such as knives, lumps of metal and broken bottles. Others described chatting with locals one minute only to be turned upon and spat at by them the next, as if some kind of signal had gone up and that the time had come for the free-for-all against the English to begin. The ensuing indiscriminate violence reached a level most found hard to comprehend as Turks of all ages and, according to those present, all social backgrounds came out and fought with Englishmen who ended up quite literally fighting for their lives. Windows were smashed, chairs and tables were sent spinning and blood began to spill in the mayhem as skulls were cracked and a reported six Englishmen stabbed. For some five minutes the violence raged on before the police came forward, adding to the chaos.

The police had been accused of wrong-footing themselves; it was suggested that they had accidentally steered the mob towards unsuspecting fans while trying to keep them away from a smaller bar containing a particular group of Leeds fans they had been tracking for most of the day. Following their late arrival they set about dispersing the fighting crowd by drawing long batons and adding their own weight to the bloodshed. A common accusation was that the Turkish officers showed a particular liking for anyone English, an argument backed up by much of the footage and first-hand accounts shown via our television screens.

There were images such as a lad with a stab-wound to his leg pleading to be left alone before being suddenly turned upon, kicked in the back and arrested. Images of a lad bleeding from the mouth, a clear victim who was not given help but was instead bundled into a waiting van. And the most disgusting image of all, of a lad desperately trying to give mouth-to-mouth to a dying man and suddenly finding himself suffering at the wrong end of a policeman's baton. All these images clearly demonstrated the fact that being an English football fan abroad can often leave you open to aggression, from all sides and of a level only those who travel can ever comprehend. The image of Christopher Loftus being bundled into a taxi is one that shall stay with English football fans forever, as will those shot hours later of his brother, leaving the hospital, shouting to the waiting cameras, 'Murdering Turkish bastards'. The unthinkable grim reality of the night's violence was hammered home in those three words. At this point all anyone could do was wait and see how the world of football would react.

Much of the focus fell on the Leeds United chairman, Peter Ridsdale. One minute Mr Ridsdale had been enjoying a meal and talking football with representatives of the Galatasaray club; the next he was involved in the nightmare of identifying bodies, facing the world's press and holding emergency talks with UEFA regarding the decision as to whether or not the game should actually go ahead. Just how you handle such a situation is almost impossible to grasp, and yet the dignity and composure shown by this man in the face of such adversity was a credit to all those he represented – the families of the victims, the city and supporters of Leeds United and this country as a whole. If only the same could be said for all the others involved. While the Turks, in particular officials of Galatasaray, were doing everything they could to disassociate themselves from the violence and steer the blame elsewhere, UEFA were busy demanding the game be played. Back home, the reaction to the night's events could not have been more different: one of the first steps taken by LUFC was to cancel all their official-supporter charter-flights, thus avoiding the risk of placing any more of their fans in danger; meanwhile most people found the fact that the match was played at all sickening, and it's a decision that to this day must be brought into question.

Surely respect for the murder victims, for their families, friends and relatives at such a time should have been the first and foremost concerns, and yet the decision was made to play a game of football before those innocent fans had even been laid to rest and their families allowed to grieve. To me, it was a disgusting decision. UEFA offered excuses that were both insulting and pathetic in the extreme: they claimed that time was too short to cancel and that to rearrange the fixture was too difficult to organise. What exactly do they mean, time was too short to cancel? Football matches are postponed at short notice the world over when snow, wind and rain bring the sport to a standstill. Fans accept that; we are not idiots. An announcement made via radio and television and the odd poster placed at the stadium easily relay the message. Were UEFA telling us that murder is somehow less of a reason, harder to justify a postponement for than the weather? The same arguments can be levelled at UEFA towards the setting of a new date and venue had the match been postponed, or was it just the fact that television schedules were in place coupled with the amount of revenue that would be lost that motivated UEFA's decision? Was money deemed to be more important than the dead bodies of two English football supporters and the devastation caused for their loved ones? Surely the green stuff doesn't rule them that much, does it?

Among the Leeds fans back home, emotions ran high. Whereas some had seen the trip to Turkey as a challenge, the prospect of violence had put off many more from travelling to the tie. And yet following the coverage of the episode both Leeds/ Bradford and Manchester airports reported an upturn in requests for flights to Istanbul from fans keen to get over to Turkey and seek out revenge. As the next day wore on the events surrounding the previous night's violence began to unfold, fuelling the anger even more. The Turks had taken it upon themselves to deport sixteen Leeds fans back to England, all of whom claimed their innocence. One of the number, a female, reported that she'd been subjected to a strip-search before having her money and jewellery stolen, her engagement ring being among the items taken. News footage showed Leeds fans afraid to leave their hotels, clearly suffering from shock. Grown men were seen with their hands, arms and heads wrapped in bandages – images that barely reflected the level of hostility they had been forced to defend themselves against. The city of Leeds fell into mourning and the Elland Road stadium was transformed into a shrine as Leeds fans found themselves joined by supporters from every corner of the country sharing their grief.

But as fans tied their tokens of condolences to the rails at the stadium, the Football Association couldn't resist airing one of their own major concerns to the media and had David Davies declare that the violence should not affect England's bid to host the 2006 World Cup finals. Personally, I found the timing and even the very mention of such an issue in relation to what had taken place both sickening and ill-advised in the extreme. To me it demonstrated beyond doubt where the true values of those that ran football lay. Surely a few day's grace to deal with the issue in hand was not too much to ask – but no, 2006, the FA's Holy Grail, the all-important money-spinning festival, had to be brought into the equation. Sickening. Desperately sickening. The failure of those at Lancaster Gate to order a minute's silence before the next weekend's fixtures was commonly regarded as yet another clear sidestep, an attempt to avoid any association between the fatal violence of Istanbul and English football back home. This failure denied all fans their right to show their respect for the loss of two fellow supporters, demonstrating once again that the gulf between Them and Us is forever widening.

And the game went on.

Outside the Ali Sami Yen stadium the streets now graced water cannons along with the tanks of the National Guard. The Leeds fans were shielded every step of the way from their coaches to the terrace by a tunnel of riot police. Once inside, their vastly reduced number were jeered by the locals and subjected to the stomach-churning vicious taunts of Turks drawing their fingers across their throats as if to imitate slashing someone's neck while the police stood by and did nothing. And then, following the two teams' arrival on to the pitch from beneath a covering of police riot-shields, came the most insulting gesture of them all; the refusal of the Turkish side to wear black armbands or hold a minute's silence as a mark of respect for those who had been murdered on their streets. I would love to have seen at that moment David O'Leary and the Leeds players turn and walk from the pitch in disgust – an impossible dream, but the gesture would have deservedly shamed Galatasaray and their fans to the whole world. The travelling English are constantly accused of having little if any respect for the cultures and values of the people whose countries they visit. Indeed, this attitude was said to be the catalyst for the trouble that flared that fateful night. But if we're talking disrespect, then surely no clearer indication of such can be found than that given by the Turkish club and certain sections of their so-called supporters at the game's commencement. There is no excuse for the stance taken by those responsible. It cannot be justified and should never, ever be forgotten.

In response, the 800 or so United fans present turned their backs on the field and stood in silence, arms out wide. Dignity, respect and sorrow for all concerned was marked out by their simple yet defiant gesture, and just how the players coped out on the pitch is something only they can tell.

The subsequent days unveiled more details of the events following the killings. It was claimed that the Turkish authorities had requested a credit-card payment for blood from the Leeds chairman; it was also alleged that death-threats had been sent through to Nigel Martyn's hotel room on the night of the murders, indicating the vastly differing values put upon the sanctity of human life. As LUFC posted a request for all Turkish fans to be refused entry to the return leg at Elland Road for the sake of everybody safety, the Turks did their best to have the game moved to a neutral country, twisting and turning to gain any advantage that might help them secure a place in the competition's final. At one stage they went as far to suggest they might take the matter to the European Court of Human Rights. When levelled against the circumstances from which it arose, such a threat was quite unbelievable, an irony obviously lost on the Turks. UEFA dragged their heels in the hope that emotions would subside, then only fuelled the fire even more by posting a fine against the Yorkshire club for the conduct of their players on the pitch rather than dealing with the Turks and their violent fans away from it.

However, the actions of UEFA should not be deemed that strange. After all, this wasn't the first time they had turned away from dealing with violent, intimidating Turkish football hooliganism. Chelsea players found themselves spat upon by hostile fans when they arrived in Turkey earlier in the season, the police offering little protection from the hordes that gather at the airport whenever a foreign team comes to town. In 1993 an estimated 200 Manchester United fans were rounded up and deported for no clear reason, while those inside the stadium were left to face a barrage of missiles as the police stood back and did nothing – until they got in on the act themselves, punching and kicking both Eric Cantona and Bryan Robson as they made their way to the dressing-room. Whereas English football constantly walks a tightrope as far as UEFA is concerned, the set of rules offered to all others appears to be far more lenient; I can't help but wonder whether the outcome would have been anywhere near the same had such violence as seen in Istanbul in April 2000 occurred in England or been instigated by English football fans. In a final show of double standards UEFA went on to demand strict reassurances from both Leeds United and the Yorkshire police regarding the safety of the Galatasaray players and officials and the small group of their fans whom they eventually allowed to attend the second leg. If only they had taken note of the previous incidents involving the Turks and requested the same such assurances prior to the match in Istanbul.

In the days building up to the return leg at Elland Road, claim and counter-claim were laid against each other in the press. Many believed the game should never have been played and that the Yorkshire club should have walked away from the event, while others argued that the Turks could not be allowed to walk into the final on the back of the two murders. The Galatasaray team arrived under an army guard, won the tie 4–2 on aggregate and moved forward to the final while their small band of fans found the hostilities levelled against them to be nothing more than a few broken coach windows. Indeed, though some had predicted an outbreak of violence reaching World War III proportions, the vast majority of Leeds supporters heeded the request from the widows of the two murdered men for them to turn their backs on revenge and so carried themselves with dignity and restraint under what must have proved quite desperate circumstances. It should also be noted that during this entire tragic episode the Leeds United chairman, Peter Ridsdale, the manager, David O'Leary, the players and all the staff at Elland Road conducted themselves in such a manner that English football shall remain forever in their debt. Theirs was a clear message to the rest of the world that the game in this country has come much further than it will be ever given credit for.

The murders of Christopher Loftus and Kevin Speight left two women widowed and four children without a father, a horrific indication of just how suddenly life can be snatched away and the world of those left behind turned upside down. May they rest in peace and may their wives and children find the strength to carry on and rebuild their lives.

3

Not-so Wonderful Copenhagen

It is the most unfortunate and yet totally unavoidable admission many of us have to face. Sometimes life throws us the harshest of lessons, offers the clearest messages and gives us undeniable indications as to what is wrong and what is right. In the cold light of day we can all sit back and take time to reflect on the positives and negatives placed before us. But when caught up in the moment, when in the thick of it and faced with an uncomfortable situation first-hand, we often regress, repeat old mistakes and fall into the same deep, dark traps we've seen before. The murders in Istanbul should have made every single football fan the world over sit back and realise once and for all that death over something as unimportant as football can never ever be justified. Nevertheless, one unwelcome legacy to arise from the fatal night of 5 April 2000 was that much of England's population and in particular its violent football followers had suddenly found themselves a whole new enemy against which to pitch their hatred. You can forget Scotland, Wales, Germany and even Argentina – for many, all that mattered now was gaining revenge over the Turks.

Galatasaray's win over Leeds pushed them forward into the final against Arsenal, to be held in the Danish capital of Copenhagen. During the build-up to the match stories of reper- cussions were mooted daily in the press, though both clubs did their best to down play the possibility of violence and further confrontation. Whereas the Galatasaray fans had established for themselves a well-tracked history of hooliganism at home matches, their fans had a much better record of behaviour when travelling. The fact that the appearance of Galatasaray in a European Cup final was to be the first ever by a Turkish side led to the club disowning themselves from the potentially violent hordes of Turkish immigrants they believed were likely to travel from all over Europe in support of the nation rather than their team – the club stated well in advance that for these supporters' actions they could not be held responsible. Arsenal, too, offered up their concerns, highlighting the notion that violent sup- porters from other English teams and in particular fans from Leeds might well travel in order to seek revenge against the Turks. Like Galatasaray, Arsenal could not be held responsible should such premonitions prove accurate. The London club took great pains to point out that up until this point their supporters had enjoyed a relatively trouble-free past both at home Euro- pean matches and especially when stepping foot upon foreign soil. Yet once the inevitable violence had erupted, pictures clearly showed that the vast majority of those fighting were donning both Galatasaray and Arsenal colours.

The Danish authorities had taken it upon themselves to adopt a low-profile approach towards policing the event. Despite all the warnings, all the evidence laid before them and the obvious tension provoked by the recent history between the English and Turkish fans, they welcomed both sets of supporters with open arms, leaving them to mingle, drink and eat with each other in the misguided hope that friendships would be forged and violence averted. To their credit, the Danish authorities had offered both sets of fans the opportunity to prove the world wrong. From a country not used to football-related violence on any large scale this was to prove a trusting but highly naïve gesture; the grim reality of their chosen strategy was that it blew up in their faces, unleashing havoc upon the usually quiet streets of their capital city.

The initial outbreak of violence reportedly took place just

before midnight and involved a mob of Galatasaray fans forming up in the main square before heading outwards towards the bars containing the Arsenal fans. Both Danish press and police came forward to back up claims made by the Arsenal supporters that it was indeed the Turks who had instigated the fighting; once it kicked off, however, the violence soon escalated into a mass brawl. Danny from Hertfordshire was present on the night and tells of his first-hand experience:

When you travel out to a big game like that it is always in the back of your mind that something might happen, but you know that usually if you want to you can avoid it and duck out of the way easy enough. You know what it's like – you're on edge and you worry about this and that. Then you get there and there's loads of Arsenal around and suddenly you're thinking, 'Oh, this'll be all right' and everything's fine. To tell the truth, at first it *was* all right, much better than I had ever thought it would be considering all the build-up in the press, and there were loads of Turks around doing their thing and getting on with it. We were all drinking and eating in the same places and for ages there wasn't a hint of trouble, not a sniff. You're thinking, 'Yeah, this is how it should be. Everyone getting on, lovely.' But as the night went on you could see the tension rising, as there were loads of young Turkish lads doing the rounds and checking out the bars. There were a few Arsenal as well, to be fair, but not really on the look-out, not in the way the Turkish lads were going about it, anyway. Then some Turks started getting mouthy out the front of the bar, and it's like, 'Here we go'. Fair play to the Arsenal, though, most turned their backs – you know, 'fuck 'em, they were only kids, wankers.' I can honestly say that most people where we were didn't want to know, but the Turks wouldn't let up. Then you hear it all kick off and there's all this noise; everyone jumps up and there's a mob of Galatasaray just going for it, mad, and they started heading straight towards where we were from the square.

It's one of those moments when it's like it's not really happening. All of a sudden you're there, stuck right in the middle of it with no way out. They started chucking bottles at the place; there's glass smashing all around you and you're ducking for cover. People are screaming but it's still like some kind of dream, not real. They were just grabbing anything they could get their hands on and throwing it. Tables, chairs, bottles! Fuck knows where they got it all from. You must have seen pictures of that bloke running along carrying a bike above his head ready to throw it at someone! Fucking madman. They're loonies, the Turks. All ages, as well – they came from everywhere to join the younger lads, blokes in their thirties and forties. Normal-looking blokes just going mental. Anything they could get their hands on, they'd use as a weapon but they fight like dogs as well. I'd never seen fighting like it.

It wasn't just people running at each other like you usually see, this was real hard-nosed fighting, people hammering the shit out of each other. Some Arsenal lads were giving just as good back, mind. It's a good job they were, else we'd have all been slaughtered. I ain't no fighter, all I wanted was to get out. There were so many people getting really badly beaten up you didn't know which way to turn. In the end you just put your head down and run. Then I saw an Arsenal lad that'd been stabbed. That was scary, really frightening. He was lying on the floor, being held by his mate, with blood dripping from his back. That's the first time I've seen someone stabbed. It's horrible, so much blood. People were shouting out to get an ambulance and trying to keep space around him. There was hardly any police around and they didn't have a clue what they were doing. Not one stopped to help him, they looked like they were shitting themselves as much as anyone. But they were so outnumbered they wouldn't have been able to do anything anyway. God knows where all the riot police were when it kicked off. I mean, they must have had some idea – a mob that big doesn't just appear from nowhere, does it!

The lad's mate was trying to keep him calm but he was shouting for help, poor bastard. What must that be like? I mean, what must have gone through his mind? You wouldn't know what to do, would you? I don't mind admitting it, when I realised he'd been stabbed I shit myself. I thought, 'He's going to die as well and I am watching it happen.' You wonder where the bastard is who did it and if you're next. All sorts of things go through your head. It's crazy, something I never want to see happen again or be near as long as I live. We just ran our way out of it; it was the most frightening situation I've ever been in by a long way. It will make me think twice about going abroad for football again. I certainly wouldn't go if we were playing a Turkish side, no way. Football isn't worth that. I only found out that the stabbed lad had lived the next day. Thank God for that. I'd spent the whole night thinking I'd seen someone get killed! I don't ever want that again.

The level of violence played out in Copenhagen's Radhuspladsen district on the night before the final clearly caught the Danish police totally unaware. Indeed the officer in charge, Superintendent Flemming Munch (a name sure to put you off your dinner), had already taken to his bed, claiming the night to be a complete success, only to be woken with the news that one Englishman had been stabbed and countless others left in need of hospital treatment. More than twenty per cent of the total Danish police force had been on duty and yet the violence was left to rage on for over ten minutes before they appeared on the scene in any real numbers and began to restore order. Despite the level of violence, fewer than ten arrests were made on the night – a figure clearly indicating that the policing was far too little too late. Unfortunately this lesson went unheeded and the Danish authorities failed to take it on board.

News of the previous night's stabbing spread quickly among

the ever-increasing number of Arsenal fans arriving in the city via the overnight trains and coaches, fuelling the hatred between the two sets of fans to unprecedented heights. By mid-afternoon the tension in the city square had reached boiling point, and yet quite amazingly in view of prior events the Danish police chose to adopt the same method of just standing back and hoping for the best. Superintendent Munch later claimed his officers had tried to carry out 'policing with a smile', but sadly at 2.15 p.m. on the afternoon of the match that smile was wiped clean from their faces.

Once again the police pointed an accusing finger in the direction of the Turkish fans, who had massed in the square and begun taunting the Arsenal supporters over the stabbing and expressing their desire for more of the same. As the tension grew so too did the number of Arsenal fans arriving in the area. Eventually, following other taunts relating to the two Istanbul murders, violence was unleashed upon the streets like never before as a mob of around 200 Arsenal fans entered the square and charged towards their Turkish counterparts. It was clear that each side had come prepared: within seconds both groups had turned the once peaceful square into a raging battleground, attacking each other with bottles, glasses, pieces of wood, tables and chairs. The Danish police, once again, seemed powerless, their dog-handlers and mounted officers a mere distraction among the frenzy taking place around them as fists flew, blood poured and skulls cracked. To the vast majority, the violent scenes were setting English football back twenty years, but to others the battle of Copenhagen was all they had expected and even hoped for, T.C. of N11 has his say:

Copenhagen was the real deal, no doubt about it. I didn't come out too good myself, but I wouldn't have missed it for the world. I haven't been involved in anything like that for years now, not that heavy. Everyone thinks the Turks are cunts now, what with the Leeds thing and all that, but fuck me do they like to row – you got to give them that at least. A lot of people have been going on about there being English lads from all over out there just to do the Turks but that's bollocks, this was Arsenal at their finest. There were other lads there, sure, but they ain't taking the credit for this, You look at the amount of Arsenal shirts doing the business next time you see that film; enough said! Like I said, I took a bit of a pasting myself – a whack around the head with a lump of something and then I got jumped – but that's the way it goes sometimes. Anyone who tells you they've never had an hiding at football and pretends to be a hooligan is a lying fucker. It's the name of the game. The bruises go in a week or two; the memory of doing a runner sticks with you for years. Me and the lads I was with had been hanging on the edge of it all day just waiting for it to go off – everyone was waiting, really. They weren't half giving it some on the Leeds thing. I tell you, they are animals, they don't give a fuck. But that really got people, that did. What a thing to wind people up over. They'll be hated forever over that. That'll never be forgotten by the English lads, that won't, and never should be.

We were well outnumbered all in all – well, they'd come from all over Europe for this, hadn't they – but when the lads steamed in it looked the fucking bollocks. Once it kicked off Arsenal came out from everywhere and it just turned into this free-for-all. All the time you're expecting the Old Bill to turn up but they shat themselves and left us to it. They should do that more often – at least we'd get it sorted out! It was fucking mad being in the thick of that, though, people just hitting whoever they found themselves standing next to. I got caught out after chasing after this geezer. He'd legged it but as soon as I stopped some bloke came at me with a piece of wood and whack, I saw it too late. It fucking hurt like buggery, right across the side of the face. If I'd have turned my head the wrong way I could have lost my eye, the way he caught me. That's scary when you think about it. I went down more out of shock at first, then it started to hurt like fuck. I thought I was in big trouble for a while but it weren't that bad in the end. But once I was down I was fucked. God knows how many of the bastards I had on me but the amount of bruises on my back that night, fucking hell! At the time I just rolled into a ball and covered my face. It went on for ages. I was thinking, 'When's some fucker going to come and help me out' but it went on and on. I think that's the worst kicking I've ever had. Still, at least I'd made one of those bastards shit himself beforehand and I'd rather have the bruises than been seen on telly back home legging it like he was. I'll put it down as a hard-fought draw.

Many of those caught up in the fighting claimed to have feared for their lives as men scoured the square in search of their next victim. The horrific image of one middle-aged Turkish fan brandishing a meat-cleaver and a pickaxe handle brought home to many the unprecedented level of violence that had been unleashed and left unchallenged, as did the disturbing pictures of one English lad lying on the tarmac with his head ripped open following an attack with an iron bar. All in all the violence raged on for almost an hour before the police entered the fray, fired their tear gas and eventually managed to gain some kind of control. In its wake the fighting had left one fan minus half an ear, another with a broken ankle and a further three nursing serious stab-wounds. The lad with the head injury was left fighting for his life in hospital while another suffered a suspected heart attack.

Following the late intervention by the police an uneasy calm descended upon the Danish capital during which only minor incidents took place. The worst of these involved Arsenal fans being escorted to the stadium who in their frustration began pulling down metal fencing. This time the police returned their aggression with a stiffer hand, drawing their truncheons and making arrests. Mercifully the match itself was completed without further disturbances. Once it was over, though, fans back home in London and Istanbul took to the streets themselves, leading to yet more bloodshed. In North London, riot police were called to quell an angry mob intent on revenge for their side's penalty shoot-out defeat. Local Turkish restaurants and kebab houses came under attack, as did the Turkish immigrant population who were driving around in their cars celebrating their team's victory. In Istanbul the mood turned sour as Galatasaray fans both celebrated their win and fought with rival fans. Nine people were shot when fans fired into the air, including a child who later died in hospital. There was still more trouble back in Denmark when rival gangs clashed at the city airport, some 200 English and Turkish fans confronting each other before police stepped in to separate them.

During two days of acrimony the Danish authorities had arrested just sixty-four people of whom only nineteen were British. All were deported and banned from returning to Denmark for a year but, much to the annoyance of the British government, not one had their name officially passed over in order that British police authorities could impose their own banning-order preventing any further travel abroad. The surprisingly low number of arrests prompted UEFA's claim that the world's media had blown the incident out of all proportion, as they desperately tried to down-play any possibility of repercussions occurring during the Euro 2000 finals. Indeed, many present in the Danish capital throughout those two days would agree with this statement. Away from the main square, fans from both sides had continued to mingle and enjoy the occasion for all it was worth – a clear suggestion that avoiding the trouble was just as easy as finding it.

Unfortunately, the images beamed around the globe told a different story. It wasn't so much the numbers involved as the level of sheer brutality witnessed that shocked the world. Copenhagen was an orgy of violence, with those caught up in it seemingly lost in the frenzy as the battle was left to rage. The pictures not only led to the Belgian police threatening strike action, but also spread fear among the people of the Low Countries. The reputation of both clubs was left in tatters, but the battle of Copenhagen and the ensuing violence in North London also made it abundantly clear that the hatred now festering between the fighting Arsenal and Galatasaray fans ran much deeper than any affinity they might have had towards their football clubs. It was a more sinister hatred, a hatred just waiting to rear its ugly head once again; and with the European Championship of 2000 just around the corner, that wait would soon be over.

4

Domestic Troubles

The turn of the century has unfortunately brought with it the strongest evidence yet that football violence is still very much alive and kicking. Three deaths, numerous stabbings, pitched battles with police and rioting both inside and outside of our new, so-called 'safe' sporting arenas have led many to believe that the dark old days are about to return with a vengeance.

One club notorious for its violent following is Cardiff City, whose fans have been at the centre of some of Great Britain's most recent confrontations. A key factor in the Welsh club's reputation is their hatred for all that is English, a hatred which is often mirrored by their opposition when their side crosses the border into St George's country. In response to Cardiff's latest visit to London, the Metropolitan Police were forced into staging their largest anti-football hooliganism operation since Euro 96 in order to keep violent City fans from clashing with the renowned Millwall FC following. However, it was Cardiff's clash with Stoke City that was to grab most of the headlines, as the level of violence displayed within the stadium shocked even the most seasoned campaigner.

Stoke City's new Britannia Stadium is without doubt an amazingly impressive arena – all that the Taylor Report recommended and more. But on the day Stoke met Cardiff there, the naïve illusion that such stadiums would prove a super-safe haven for the football fan was totally shattered. Given the well-documented hooligan followings attached to both teams, the clash of the two city sides was always going to be a tense encounter, but with Stoke fighting for a play-off place and Cardiff struggling to avoid relegation the fire was given added fuel. In the build-up to the game the Internet had been awash with threats and counter-threats, although just how much of this was down to sad, spotty teenagers sitting in their bedrooms rather than the work of hardcore hooligans is always open to debate. However, on the day, the Welsh fans travelled in their thousands and brought with them a cache of weapons big enough to arm a small-island race out in the Pacific, with the array including more than a hundred Stanley blades and a circular saw.

The whistle blown by the referee to start the game also signalled the start of the violence within the stadium as the home fans clashed with stewards and police in their attempt to get into the away section. The sudden arrival of several hundred Cardiff latecomers following a drinking session in nearby Stafford provoked many of those Welsh fans already in the ground into retaliation as they began to rip out the seats, surge forward and send their newly found arsenal hurling into the home stand. The sudden upturn in violence then forced police in full riot gear into action, but their baton-charge of the Welsh fans only intensified their aggression because many felt they had been targeted while the home fans had been left to their own devices. Mounted police were then bought into the fray, lining up in front of the Cardiff fans before finding themselves the target of yet more missile-throwing. Their presence also led to the bizarre sight of player Andy Legg having to ask one of them to move in order for him to take a corner kick. Once outside, the violence erupted yet again as Stoke fans attempted to rip down fencing surrounding the away fans' coach-park in the hope of reaching their enemy, their actions resulting in vicious fighting with the police who did their best to keep the two groups apart. Unfortunately the Cardiff hooligans responded by climbing the fences and launching an attack of their own, and so the authorities found it coming at them from all angles. All this in a country claiming to be at the forefront of anti-hooligan measures.

Indeed, during the season leading up to Euro 2000, Division Two played host to a number of major incidents when some of the most vicious firms in the country found themselves thrown into opposition. And one name that shall forever ring the worry bells is, of course, Millwall FC. It should be put on record that the London club has taken tremendous strides forward over recent years. Those that run the club have been doing everything in their power to rid the Lions of their tarnished image, but regrettably when the going gets tough the tough turn out for the lads from the New Den – and last year they turned out on more than one occasion. The two fixtures with Cardiff provided more than a few headaches for the police and for those caught up in the troubles, while Millwall's trip to Burnley witnessed the London fans ripping out wooden seating before showering it down upon the playing-surface in their efforts to force the game's abandonment.

The end of Millwall's most successful season on the pitch for some time saw them reach the play-offs where they were drawn to meet Wigan Athletic, a side with a much smaller but nonetheless handy little firm of their own. The first leg, played down at the New Den, ended in a 0–0 draw leaving the London club playing the role of the underdog as they headed north for the second leg. Just 600 Wigan fans braved the trip to the New Den, a figure that surely reflects the level of hostility some still expect to receive when travelling to Millwall. In contrast, some 4000 Londoners made the opposite journey, many of whom travelled on free transport provided by the Millwall chairman, Theo Paphitis, doing all he could to give his side the best possible opportunity to overturn the odds stacked against them. However, the fans' gratitude was not shared by the Lancashire constabulary, whose worst fear came crashing home when a 1–0 defeat led to 4000 unhappy Londoners and landed them with one hell of a problem.

What made things worse for many of the Millwall fans present that night was the fact that they had played the home side off the park. At the final whistle, the jubilant home fans stormed the pitch and taunted their rivals over the defeat and their shattered dream of a trip to Wembley's twin towers. As the tension grew, police in riot gear chased the Wigan fans from the pitch while Millwall fans ripped out seats from the new JJB Stadium's away end and threw coins at their rivals. The police set about dispersing the home fans from outside the ground, but Millwall fans inside became agitated at being held back and yet more violence followed. Riot police with truncheons then clashed with the Londoners, splitting heads and spilling blood while the fans kicked and punched back in the hope of getting out of the stadium and into the home supporters, who were busy stoning the Millwall supporters' coaches. All in all, it was a sorry day for both clubs, but with Wigan losing the play-off final to Gillingham the two are set to meet again and hostilities will no doubt be reignited.

It is not just within the top four divisions that violence rears its head. This the supporters of Conference side Nuneaton Borough would be only too quick to point out following their visit from Hereford United in March 2000. Police 'intelligence' prior to the game had offered information that just 150 Hereford fans were expected to make the journey across the Midlands in order to attend the match, but tension in the town before kick-off suggested that the police had got these figures well and truly wrong. It soon became clear that a good few of those who had made the journey were on the lookout for the local 'boys' as they went from pub to pub in search of the Nuneaton lads who had over recent years built a bit of a reputation of their own. With that in mind, many home fans entering the ground voiced their concerns regarding the lack of both police on duty and segregation between the home 'Cock and Bear' end and the usual away stand known as the 'Canal side'. Eventually the inevitable happened when, in a throwback to the 70s and 80s, a firm of around thirty Hereford hooligans steamed across to 'take' the home end, kicking and punching all who got in their way. What shocked most people was not just the mindless, indiscriminate violence but also the ages of those involved – many appeared to be well into their late thirties and forties. Grown men still living in the dark ages and offering undisputable proof that football violence doesn't diminish following the loss of League status.

However, the most tragic event to occur on these shores during the 1999–2000 season came at the Third Division championship decider between Rotherham United and Swansea City, a match which ended with yet another death to add to the Istanbul murders of just a month earlier. With the home side needing to win in order to wrestle the championship trophy from the visitors' grasp, United's Millmoor Stadium played host to a sell-out crowd. The police had considered the match to be of high risk, so had deployed more than 115 officers on to the streets – many of whom soon found themselves dealing with sporadic outbreaks of violence and drunken hooliganism. As hostility rose, the police set about the task of escorting fans away from the pubs and into the stadium. Nevertheless, at 2.30 p.m. tragedy struck when a group of Swansea fans came under attack from United fans throwing bottles, bricks and cans from a nearby pub. As some City fans began to return the fire, mounted police-horses charged forward to separate the rival fans. Amid the ensuing hysteria many innocent supporters were caught up in disturbances. One such person was Swansea fan Terry Coles. Accounts differ as to what actually happened; however it was reported that he was trampled by a frightened horse in a moment of chaos that left him with a fractured skull and fatal internal injuries. During the match that followed, fans invaded the pitch twice and the day saw nineteen people arrested. Most importantly, once again, two children found themselves left without a father.

Terry Coles was clearly a football fan rather than a hooligan. Many claimed that they had seen him trying to stop people from joining in the missile-throwing at the time of the tragic incident. The next day, one fan was prompted into leaving a card outside Swansea's Vetch Field Stadium. Inside was the inscription: 'Another senseless death at the hands of the South Yorkshire police' – a poignant reminder of the Hillsborough disaster and the local constabulary's past. Out of respect for Terry Coles, his family and all who knew him, Swansea City cancelled their planned civic reception and subsequent celebrations. Let us hope that a full explanation of what happened is eventually made, and that justice is seen to be done.

T.C. may you rest in peace.

5

It's a Big Bad World Out There

The incidents outlined in the previous chapter relate purely to violence within the English domestic set-up, but it is not just the self-confessed home of football violence that finds itself caught in the hooligans' grip as we hit the new millennium. It is true to say that of the countries competing at Euro 2000, only England, Turkey, Germany, Yugoslavia and the Czech Republic posed any real threat of bringing violence along to the party with them, as it is only these countries that have a real reputation for hooliganism when travelling away on international duty. However, on the domestic front the story is very different indeed, and the football hooligan continues to cast a shadow over the beautiful game worldwide.

In the season building up to Euro 2000 the hooligans were hard at it. In Italy one policeman was left in a coma and five others injured after violence flared between fans of local rivals Bari and Lecce. On the same weekend an estimated 200 Cagliari fans stormed their teams' dressing-room following the side's relegation from the top flight before turning on the police who were forced into firing tear gas in order to quell the mob. During the 1999–2000 season, Serie A also witnessed an upturn in racist propaganda within its stadiums, with the Rome club Lazio coming in for most of the criticism. Banners such as the ones seen were made illegal in the mid-nineties following the murder by AC Milan fans of a Genoa supporter, but by smuggling in the abusive statement letter-by-letter Lazio fans found a way of beating the ban and sending their message to the world. Racist undertones were also behind the fatal stabbing in Spain of a Real Sociedad supporter in December 1998 by an Atletico Madrid hooligan who was later sentenced to seventeen years' imprisonment. In Romania, hooligan supporters of Dinamo Bucharest ripped apart the away end and hurled more than eighty seats on to the pitch during a fixture with Rapid, whose fan-base is considered to be predominately made up of gypsies (a race never at the top of the Christmas-card list in that neck of the woods) and has therefore come under increasing attack from all sides this season. In Belgrade, Yugoslavia, a teenage fan died as a result of violent clashes involving Partizan's notorious 'Gravediggers' firm and fans of Red Star; while across the border the Croatian Cup final first-leg between Dynamo Zagreb and Hajduk Split had to be abandoned with four minutes remaining when police released tear gas into the crowd to separate rival fighting mobs.

Another derby game making the headlines for all the wrong reasons occurred in the Hungarian capital of Budapest, where Ferencvaros and Ujpest fans fought pitched battles that saw fifty people injured and twelve arrested. Hooliganism is currently threatening to bring Hungarian football to its knees as crowds drop to all-time lows, something clearly demonstrated by the fact that recent television footage showing one Ferencvaros lout attacking a pensioner not only shocked the nation but saw the club's attendances halve almost overnight. Most English fans will tell you that Poland can be an iffy place to visit, and the country has indeed seen a continued escalation in football violence. There, the anti-terrorist squad were called in to counter violent clashes between supporters of Widzew Lodz and Legia Warsaw – the second time in less than eight months that the elite force had been brought in to quell aggressive crowds. Meanwhile in St Petersburg, Russia, a fan lost his life during violent street-rioting. And the list goes on. Across the Atlantic, two fans received gunshot wounds during clashes between the Brazilian sides Vasco da Gama and Flamengo, the violence sparked by a mass five-minute brawl among the players. In Liberia riot police were forced to beat back fans with batons as an estimated 50,000 tried to cram themselves into a stadium built for 33,000. Three fans were crushed to death in the panic. For real turmoil, however, head back north to Greece – for within their domestic set-up it's not just the players, fans and police who cause the problems. Here, the trouble goes right to the boardroom.

Olympiakos are currently the top team in Greek football and attached to them is a hooligan following to match. The feud their supporters have with fans of rivals AEK Athens borders on the insane, as the stones, wood and petrol bombs thrown at coaches carrying AEK fans to a recent fixture show. This attack was sparked by fighting the previous week between the two groups of fans at a basketball match, but it pales into insignificance when compared to an incident that took place in the AEK boardroom earlier in the season. At the time, Victor Mitropolous was the chairman of the Greek League and a man under intense pressure. His popularity within the game is so low that armed bodyguards are never far from his side – and not without good reason. Following a rather heated disagreement with someone, his minder was stabbed and five gunshots were fired, but although the incident was caught on camera not one person had been charged at the time of writing. The vice-chairman of the League was also caught in the crossfire during an earlier gunfight, and accusations of corruption and bribery sweep through the corridors of the top Greek clubs. Indeed, in a recent poll more than sixty per cent of fans stated a belief that the Greek Championship is decided away from the pitch rather than on it. This belief led to three top clubs – AEK's Nikolaides, Atmatsides and Kassapis – boycotting the national side in protest.

Allegations of match-fixing and the nobbling of officials are as common as Frenchmen demanding transfers. In 1995 the Greek cup final referee was ambushed and beaten, while during the 1998–1999 season a top referee was shot six times in the legs – incidents that make a stand-off with Roy Keane look like a child's birthday party. Away from the pitch, the fans battle on relentlessly despite their rapidly diminishing numbers. Eight people were arrested and numerous others injured when Olympiakos Pireaus fans fought a pitched battle with supporters of Aris Salonika aboard a ferry taking them to a recent First Division fixture. The fighting continued long after the fans had disembarked, leaving behind a trail of damaged vehicles, cracked heads and injured bystanders.

While such a level of corruption and violence seems a million miles away from our own supposedly squeaky clean domestic leagues, you have to take into account the fact that European competitions and World Cup qualifiers more often than not have that rather annoying habit of throwing up those fixtures and away trips you have been so desperately trying to avoid – as was so clearly demonstrated when the draw for Euro 2000's play-off fixtures pitched England and Scotland together in a two-legged head-to-head.

Following England's relatively trouble-free group matches, this was the draw everyone feared as it promised not only to open old wounds but also cast a huge shadow over the England fans in the build-up to the finals should they qualify. Both the English and Scottish Football Associations, together with the police on both sides of the border, went into overdrive as they set about the biggest police operation Glasgow had witnessed for some fifteen years in order to ensure the first leg of the tie went off peacefully. All police leave was cancelled as threat and counter-threat spread via the Internet for what was suddenly being billed as the battle of the century. For the English hooligan there is no greater challenge than a trip to Glasgow, as for them the memory of the great Scottish invasion of England in 1977, during which the Tartan Army came, saw, conquered and virtually demolished both Wembley and the West End of London still hurts to the bone. Since the abolition of the Home International competition, opportunities for the English hooligans to take some form of revenge have been few and far between, whereas for their Scottish counterparts the mere mention of

'77 is all they need offer as, since that fateful day, they believe it has been up to the English to come forward and reclaim the crown!

Despite all the pre-match hype, the game passed off without any real major incident. The English turned up, but in numbers nowhere near those that were predicted. For those who did show there were few real moments to remember, other than the odd charge up the road interspersed by a hail of bottles aimed towards those Scots who had turned up to defend their turf. Whereas the English claimed a small victory in the fact that they had turned out, the Scottish hooligans countered their claim by pointing out that just about anybody can be brave when standing behind line after line of coppers. In truth it was the police who won the day hands down. By shadowing the two firms' every move and hemming them into various bars situated in the city centre, the police kept the confrontation down to a minimum, proving that when they get their tactics right, the problem can be dealt with relatively easily.

PART TWO
Portugal

———————————

6

You Better Get a Move On, Boy

Wednesday 7 June 2000

The ring of my mobile phone has me jumping to my feet and
reaching for the handset:

'Hello'.

'Hello. Is that the Gay-Vicars-Looking-Up-an-Old-Friend
Chatline?' Such a question could only come from one person.

'Ah, Mr Wiltshire of the West Country Fist-Fucking Bungee-
Jumping Club, I presume?'

'Yes, it is I.'

I first met Wiltshire during France 98 when I was videoing a
mob of locals who had just attacked the café I had hoped to get
pissed in. While they were throwing petrol bombs at the remaining English, Wiltshire was threatening to kick my head in and
shove the camera up my arse if I didn't stop! Funny how things
turn out, isn't it? Despite our unusual introduction Wiltshire
and I have been distant friends ever since. I like Wiltshire – not
in that 'any port in a storm, we all look the same with the lights
off' way so accepted by the boys from his neck of the woods,
but because he's a chancer and a fucking good laugh. Believe
me, if there's any chance of a scam Wiltshire's probably already
invented it. Out in France, I didn't see him pay for one train
journey. He blagged hotels and paid for things only as a last

resort – except for beer, of course, which he always felt was value for money. One thing I did learn during the World Cup is that there are an awful lot of blokes like Wiltshire. Blokes who are up for anything but who like to travel out alone for one reason or another and make their acquaintances once they have safely arrived at the destination of the match.

This telephone call couldn't have come at a better time: I'd been trying to contact Wiltshire for the last few weeks because I had held the notion of maybe travelling out to Holland in his company. Unfortunately, though, his arrangements had already been made and, as ever, he was planning to go it alone. One thing the conversation made me realise was that I was making my usual mistake of leaving everything until the last minute; so, once I had put the phone down, I finally decided to get my arse in gear.

My first task is obvious: I need to get myself out there. But I soon find out that leaving it late is going to cost. Easyjet: £117 one-way! (So much for the £50 deal.) Ryan Air: £112. Eurostar: £240! Yes, honestly! Suddenly it's looking more than a little bit naughty. I check out the bus from Victoria. It's only £45 return but that has got to be a last resort. I had really hoped to arrive in Amsterdam on the Sunday in time for when the Dutch play the Czechs at the Amsterdam Arena, but if I go by coach it will mean travelling overnight with a busload of stoners and e-heads for company. Marvellous. Now I am even thinking about taking the car. At least that way I would be guaranteed somewhere to sleep. I begin to look up the price of ferries when suddenly something catches my eye: the Stena-Line Holland Express. Sounds good – 8.45 train from Liverpool Street station up to Harwich. Over to the Hook and arriving in Amsterdam just in time for tea, all for just £76 return. Lovely jubbly! I do the business, put the phone down and then it hits home: I am off to Euro 2000! Suddenly I am not scared anymore. All those nagging worries kicked to dust by thoughts of Amsterdam and yet another great football experience. Now all I need is someone to go with – and one name immediately springs to mind.

I've known Keef since the year dot. We grew up together,

went to school together and started following football together. I hate to admit it, but it was Keef's brother and his mates from Hemel Bumstead that first got me into trouble at football. They were a nasty bunch of bastards, but as an impressionable teenager I quickly found myself wanting to be part of it all, one of the lads, accepted. As for Keef, well, a funnier bloke and better mate you would struggle to find. He looks like a bit of a nutter, and though he does suffer at the hands of the old red mist it takes a fair bit to get him going – unless, of course, he's been drinking, then he can be a right stroppy bastard. He is also a sexual deviant; a pervert of the highest order. If asked: 'Would you shag a fifteen-year-old?' Keef would undoubtedly reply: 'A fifteen-year-old what?' And therefore I can't think of a better man with whom to travel to Amsterdam. Nevertheless, it's going to take the hard sell. I pick up the phone and fill him in on the plan:

'Ed, don't do this to me. You know I'm skint.'

'Yeah, I know. But Keef, it's a one-off, a chance of a lifetime.'

'Yeah, but my bird won't see it that way, will she? They don't think like blokes, do they!' Desperation begins to creep into his voice and now I know I am on a winner.

'Go on, Keef, you know it makes . . .'

'Fuck off.' There is a short pause and I can hear the argument with his girlfriend already being played out in his mind. 'Ed, I ain't saying yes, right. But I'll ring you tomorrow. Oh, and Ed, you're a cunt for doing this!' I put the phone down, clap my hands: job done!

Later that day the news comes through that two known English hooligans have been deported, the first of the tournament. One was stopped at Amsterdam's Schipol airport, the other when getting off the ferry at the Hook of Holland.

7

We're All Going to Die!

Thursday 8 June

The news of the two deportations seems to have kicked the English press into overdrive. Headlines from the sports pages proclaim such things as the *Mirror*'s: 'BELGIANS FEAR CARNAGE'; '1 MATCH & 2 MORGUES'. They refer to the fact that the Belgian authorities, following on from what happened in Istanbul, have prepared themselves for the worst-case scenario by setting up two mortuaries in the town of Charleroi, one for English fans and one for the Germans. This has been done in order to keep grieving families apart should everybody's greatest fears come to fruition. It's an article that has the old bum twitching, and once again those nagging worries start banging on in my head. What the hell is going on? England are playing Germany at football and they actually believe people might get killed. I sit and think about that for a minute. Surely any rational person would suggest that if that is the case, then the game should simply not be played. It's only a football match, for Christ's sake! Were there the possibility of someone getting killed at any event other than a football match, the government, safety officers and police would step in and ban it without hesitation. Fact! Surely the events in Istanbul proved without any shadow of a doubt that the result of a football match means nothing compared to the loss of life – absolutely nothing. And yet here we are, just a few months later, obviously having learned nothing. I start to question my own sanity, and tell myself that at the first sign of trouble I'll be heading straight back home.

An item on the midday news adds to my concern. We are shown pictures of workmen converting disused garages into mass holding-pens capable of storing up to seventy-five prisoners. The police are also releasing the country's low-risk prisoners for the weekend in order to create more space for the expected influx of football thugs. The item also contains an interview with a Turkish bar-owner who states that he will welcome the English but if punched he will fight back. The interview does nothing but produce a good sound bite for the interviewer, highlight the bleeding obvious and throw yet another coal on the fire. Well done. The respected British press are already rubbing their hands together at the prospect of the year's top story.

Also on the news is an item which while being far from threatening is disturbing nonetheless. It revolves around the England players preparing to set off for Belgium looking more like a bunch of bingo-callers off on a family shindig than a group of highly paid international footballers. They are wearing cheap suits and shirts with collars so large even Harry Hill would not be seen dead in them. Maybe it's a safety measure just in case the plane starts to go down. Who knows. One other rather funny story is the confession made today by the Swedish player Freddie Ljungberg following a sex-ban being imposed on the Swedish team by their coach. Freddie is delighted at the news because his feet apparently go numb after a spot of the old in and out! I can't help thinking he must be doing something wrong – either that or he knows a new trick not even Keef has heard of yet.

Meanwhile, King Kev has tried to rally the country by banging his chest to the rhythm of: 'We're going out to win.' It's a battle-cry that immediately has the pen-pushers slating the chances of both the manager and the team. What is it with our press, eh? All right, so we made it through the back door but at least we made it. Ask the jocks what they would rather be doing.

Exactly. OK, so Kev wears his heart on his sleeve, but God, does he mean it. You know every defeat hurts him like it hurts the rest of us. He never hides his feelings, his pride at being English. His enthusiasm breeds hope, and yet they pick away at him, try to wear him down and hunt out his every weakness at just the time when the country needs the man at the top to feel that everybody is behind him. Why shouldn't everybody share his belief that we actually have a chance of winning Euro 2000 and aren't there just making up the numbers? Keegan often asks our pressmen the question, 'Whose side are you on?' shaking his head in disbelief and despair at some of the idiotic, irrelevant interrogation directed his way. And yet despite the pressure, despite the media hammering away at him, Keegan nearly always comes out of the situation with his dignity intact. Whenever the man is interviewed you know he is answering the question exactly how he sees it. As a supporter what more could you ask for? It would be hard to imagine a more polite man, gracious in both victory and defeat – qualities many a Premiership manager couldn't even comprehend let alone put into practice. Kevin Keegan is a manager willing to give everything, and he'll give it in public. Of course, this lays him open to attack, but I love his foot-in-the-mouth comments and his appalling predictions. They make him human, real and like the rest of us. Keegan wants success for the players, for the country, for the fans. He wants it so badly. With Keegan you know what you're getting. It's all done in the hope of getting it right. It's heartfelt and honest – words and sentiments lost on many of those who scrutinise his every decision. As the team head off to Belgium, I for one am glad that the man at the head of it all is out there doing it for every single one of us. He *is* one of us, a man well and truly on our side; if only the press could find it within themselves to come down on his side.

The day ends on a couple of high notes. Keef rings to tell me he has booked the ferry, and I get a shag!

8

Absolutely Spliffing

Friday 9 June 2000

Today is amazingly quiet on the news-front considering the big kick-off is just a day away. This may be down to the fact that three men arrested in a Brussels park carrying hunting knives and a crossbow actually turned out to be reporters from the *News of the World*. Upon being nicked they'd tried to explain that they were simply working on an undercover story about the ease with which such weapons can be bought on the continent. However, their excuse doesn't stop them spending the night in the cells. Cells that will no doubt be branded 'HELL-HOLE PRISON AWAITING ENGLISH SCUM THUGS' etc., etc. come Sunday morning.

The English police have also been busy, taking to court and gaining restriction orders on thirty-six known hooligans, most of whom are based in the North East. The head of the police's National Criminal Intelligence Service (NCIS)'s football unit, Bryan Drew, is out and about and clocking up the overtime. He appears on almost every news programme telling us that his unit have passed over to their Dutch and Belgian counterparts a thousand names and addresses of people whom they believe will be travelling to the tournament with the intention of causing trouble. I can't help but think we'll be seeing a lot of

Bryan over the next few weeks. Once again, the same old warnings are being dragged out of the bin in the hope of fooling the public. Home Office Minister Lord Bassam trots out the time-honoured favourite about zero tolerance and how they will impose a ten-year ban from every football ground on anyone caught stepping out of line. Unfortunately most of the names and addresses that have been handed over belong to known hooligans who are, by their own admission, already serving such bans. The words door, horse and bolted spring to mind.

As the world's press focus their attention on the issue of hooliganism, one major story has almost slipped by unnoticed. It transpires that while the whole of Europe has been worrying about the tournament's criminal turn-out, the Yugoslavian nation has been on tenterhooks waiting to hear whether its heroes would even get to kick a ball. Kosovo-Albanian associations in Belgium and Holland had sought to halt the Yugoslavs' entry into the countries, claiming that the team would be acting as representatives of Slobodan Milosevic. Had the court judged in the groups' favour, the Yugoslav football team would have been refused entry under an EU resolution banning such representation, something that would have thrown the competition's organisers into chaos. As if they didn't have enough problems already.

While I'm packing my bags, news comes through that Amsterdam's local politicians have passed the extreme measure of banning the wearing of balaclavas in the city for the duration of the tournament. (And there I was, going through my old junior-school bag hunting out one of my mum's finest . . .) Meanwhile there are people who wholeheartedly believe that the city of Amsterdam already has at its disposal the ultimate tool for combating the problem of hooliganism, as well as the means to put their theory into practice: marijuana.

Davy, football fan, mate of mine and regular tripper to the Dam, explains how he would deal with any trouble should it rear its ugly head:

What they should do is roll a spliff of Zeppelin-size

proportions and have it on stand-by at the airport. Then if any trouble starts they should send it up, light one end and just keep it circling overhead until everyone calms down, chills out and starts having a laugh. Think I'm taking the piss? Well you tell me the last time you saw someone looking for a fight with a spliff in their hand? You can't be arsed to turn the telly over let alone argue with someone. The Dutch police should have them on hand instead of truncheons. If anyone looks like they are getting out of hand they should go up to them, spark one up and go, 'Have a tug on that.' Two minutes later they've got a new best mate – problem sorted.

I know, it's a crazy plan – but boy, wouldn't you just love to see them give it a go! I tell you what, I'll even offer myself up for a trial run. How's that?

9

Tickets, Please

The big day for Euro 2000 has arrived, the waiting is over so let the battle commence. Well, Belgium are playing Sweden, anyway! Still there's fuck all else on the telly, so I might as well get into the spirit of things and get myself down the pub. Like on most opening days, there seems to be an air of anticlimax. Prompted by an item published in the *Daily Mail*, I've wasted most of the day on the Internet trying to track down match tickets which it claimed were available. Up until now the thought of buying tickets in advance hadn't even entered my mind. Not being a member of the Official England Supporters' Club means that I, along with probably around 10,000 others, shall be relying on both the inefficiency of the organisers and the England fans' greatest friend, the ticket tout, if I am to have even the slightest hope of attending any of the England games.

The *Mail*'s story broke following an exposé by the German Interior Minister Otto Schily who felt that the British government had failed to impose enough restrictions on known English hooligans. Otto had managed to buy tickets from agencies in both London and Bournemouth – tickets that were originally bought in the so-called 'blind ballot' before finding their way into the agencies' hands. They were now selling them at ten times their face-value and didn't even know for which part of the ground they were allocated. Schily also found a company based in America which had tickets for the England v Germany game, priced at £800. The company in question I remember well from France 98. All this points to the fact that once again those who run football couldn't organise a gang-bang at a brothel, but it also suddenly reminds me of a lad I met at Vicarage Road on the last day of the season.

While we watched my beloved WFC dick Coventry City 1–0, the guy sitting next to my mate Jeff suddenly turned and asked him whether he knew of anyone who wanted tickets for the England v Portugal game. My ears pricked up; I took his number and he told me to give him a ring in a week or so because he was off to Egypt on business. Like a prat I had forgotten to make the call – until now.

'Sorry, mate, the England tickets have gone, but I've got Germany v Romania tickets if you're interested?'

'Well, that's no good – England are playing on the same day.'

'Yeah, I know, everyone says that. I've got tickets for Italy v Sweden as well. I'll do them at £60 each. That'll be a good game, that one.'

'Sorry, mate, not interested. But if you don't mind me asking, how much did you get for the England tickets?'

'England? £400 the pair.' There is a pause. 'Tell you what, I'll do the Italy tickets for £50 each. I can't say fairer that – they're £45 tickets face-value. If you want them my partner over in Chesham has them. I'm off to Africa tomorrow on business and won't be back for three weeks.'

Now, my immediate reaction to the conversation was this: what the fuck is a guy in Chesham doing with a fistful of Euro 2000 tickets, tickets he has absolutely no intention of using? I can't help thinking that there is probably some poor German having the same conversation with a bloke in Moenchengladbach. Only, he's getting offered England tickets or the chance of a lifetime to see Yugoslavia play Slovenia. Still, every cloud has a silver lining, and once my disappointment had faded I realised that if this guy had spares over here then the black market for tickets over the water should be nicely buoyant.

In their desperation to find a violent angle the *Daily Mail* surpasses itself, pulling out all the stops and declaring that Lord's Cricket Ground is on alert fearing a hooligan invasion! Apparently security has been stepped up for the day's Benson and Hedges Cup final after a tip-off suggested that Bristol City football hooligans following Gloucestershire might clash with Cardiff City hooligans following Glamorgan! Couldn't it just be that cricket has its own problem? Do they have to pin every incident on to football? This is journalism at its worst: lazy, boring and full of shite.

Back in the real world, the opening game turns out to be a cracker. Great goals, a fair bit of controversy and a goalkeeping blunder we'll all be seeing for years. The Swedes get beaten 2–1 by the host nation, a result which sends my outside bet for the tournament winners straight down the toilet. Within the stadium there are a surprising number of empty seats, something that once again has me at my most optimistic. But the highlight of the match has to be the sight of Freddie Ljungberg going down with cramp! Obviously all that talk of a sex ban was nothing more than a load of old wank, if you'll pardon the pun! Also during the match the Belgian police got their first high-profile result of Euro 2000, when they arrested two muggers who stole match tickets from a Swedish fan just hours before. They managed to spot the thieves by the ingenious method of scouring the Scandinavian supporter's section and spotting the bandits' dark hair among a mass of Swedish blond! Now, even I'll admit that was clever.

10

Sexshe, Sexshe Ladies, Yes?

Sunday 11 June 2000

At last the day has arrived for me to set sail for Holland. I check the news on TV and see a slightly surprised journalist reporting that all is quiet on the eastern front and that the English fans are, well . . . scratch of the head . . . *behaving* themselves! In his voice you detect an air of: 'Blimey, I am not here for this, they should be kicking things off by now! Still, give it a few more hours and I'll be back.' Tosser. Later, while driving into London, the news is slightly different. A radio bulletin reports trouble between Belgium fans and the riot police in Brussels following last night's match; apparently police used water cannons and tear gas to disperse the crowd. On hearing this my wife pipes up: 'Imagine if they were English fans? I bet *that* would have been all over the TV news.'

She has obviously been living with me for far too long. One other item to crackle through states that any person claiming unemployment benefit or social security and spotted out at the finals will have their claim stopped as part of a government crackdown on benefit fraud. That's nice, that is – not only are these people unemployed; they're also expected to live a miserable existence. Yeah, nice one, Tony and your caring, sharing government!

At Liverpool Street I say my goodbyes to my wife and head off feeling a little troubled by the fact that she seems quite glad to see the back of me. When I went to France it was all tears and snot. This time it's all smiles, a Benny Hill-style pat on the head and 'Off you go, then', which is more than a little worrying! Oh well, I suppose I'll have to check the itemised phone bills again . . . Still, once out of sight out of mind: now it's time to find Keef.

I spot him a mile off. He's grinning from ear to ear and looking *very* excited. He has only ever been to one England game and that was at Wembley some years back, so this trip is going to provide him with a whole new experience. Although he mainly followed Watford with me when he was younger, his heart has always been with Fulham because of his dad and the fact that his dog came from down that way! Seems like as good a reason as any I suppose. In fact, I owe his dad big time, because on numerous occasions he took us both down to Craven Cottage to see George Best and Rodney Marsh play. (And yes, those two players really were as good as everybody says they were.) Thankfully Keef has never really been one for football violence, and has only started to get back into the game after years of neglecting it. In order to persuade Keef to come to Holland, I made an agreement with him that at the first sign of trouble we would drink up and move on to another bar – like me, all he wanted to do was to have a beano in Amsterdam and not hang around where things could turn nasty.

One incident that I think turned Keef away from football and saved him from getting involved in trouble at matches much later in life occurred one winter at Oxford United's Manor Ground. The whole pitch was covered in snow and really the game should never have gone ahead. Throughout the match the Old Bill were being pelted with snowballs, something that was obviously pissing them right off; and then at the final whistle certain sections from both sets of fans steamed on to the pitch in order to have a go at each other. I know it's hard to believe, but back then Oxford's ground was even more of a shithole than it is now because at that time they didn't even have that tiny little side stand where the away fans sit. All there was for away fans was the usual away end, a small bit of open terrace joined on to a covered terrace section housing home supporters along the side. While the police were doing their best to keep people off the pitch, Keef and I climbed over the small fence separating the home and away fans on that side terrace. In hindsight this was not the best of plans, as the Oxford lads out on the pitch were by now well on top and looking further afield. I remember getting myself back over the fence quicker than Arsene Wenger could have thought up an excuse, but Keef was nowhere to be seen. Ten minutes later I was enjoying the safety of the supporters' coach when suddenly, from out of the alley that runs along the back of the stand, Keef appeared, being chased by a small group of United fans. Every one of them was struggling to keep their balance on the icy pavement, their legs and arms flying everywhere, in fair impression of ducks landing on a frozen pond. Though from where I was sitting the whole scene looked hysterical, Keef's face was etched with horror. Thankfully he managed to get on board untouched, but I am sure the incident was a little too close for comfort and made him think twice about any future involvement.

Back at Liverpool Street station I notice the concourse is full of blokes who are obviously waiting for the same train as us. One thing immediately strikes me: unlike everyone else, neither Keef nor I are carrying any luggage. We agree that this could actually be a mistake, perhaps giving the impression that we don't really think we're going to be staying long, or even expect to get through the passport checks in the first place. The one thing Keef has brought is a quite ridiculous hat that makes him look like some kind of West Country window-licker, although through gritted teeth I tell him he looks the dog's bollocks! Keef remarks that most of those waiting for the train look like right nasty bastards, to which I reply, 'Welcome to England away!'

We collect our tickets and board the packed 8.45 train to Harwich. The mood on this journey out is quiet, probably owing to a mixture of Sunday-morning hangovers and worried anticipation about what might be waiting for us on our arrival at the ferry terminal. Although there is no reason for either Keef or me to be refused entry, we can't help feeling it's somehow going to happen. It's like when you're coming through customs and though you're carrying nothing but the right amount of duty-free you still feel guilty as hell. Once inside the ferry terminal we see that the place is crawling with British soldiers. It all seems a bit over the top until we realise they are really only toy soldiers, Territorial Army tossers off on some half-arsed exercise. The TA crack me up: a mix of spotty teenagers, young girls who are not yet sure of their sexuality and middle-aged men with beer-guts and moustaches. It looks more like a scene from *Bilko* than *Rambo* and I can't help thinking that if this is the best back-up we've got should the Germans decide to have another pop, then we all might as well start cooking pretzels.

While standing in the queue, paranoia creeps in and I convince myself that the copper standing to one side of me is giving me the once-over, when in truth he is probably bored shitless and staring into space. We collect our boarding passes then turn towards passport control, where our progress suddenly comes to an abrupt halt and the fun begins. As promised, everyone is to have their passport taken and their name checked and, as ever, the organisation involved is pathetic: just two blokes, one laptop and 200 England fans! Oh, and the ferry leaves in . . . fifteen minutes! We suddenly start to notice some worried faces. People begin biting their nails and huddling in corners.

As the English fans wait, all the foreign passengers are ushered through unchecked, and Keef hatches a cunning plan. We seem to be the only two blokes not wearing any England colours, so he suggests trying to convince the immigration officer that we are not football fans at all but rather a couple of arse bandits heading off to Amsterdam for some heavy boy-on-boy industrial hardcore bum-action. It's a good idea so I hand over my passport and the questions begin.

'Are you going to the football?'

'Yes.' *Doh.*

'Have you got any tickets or hotels booked?'

'No.' *Doh.*

'Stand over there.'

Sorry but with so many sailors around I'd rather be refused entry . . . pardon the pun!

One thing I find quite worrying is the fact that once your name has been checked on the laptop they take your passport off behind closed doors to do God knows what with it. For all we know, our names and addresses could be finding themselves added on to some NCIS file as potential trouble-makers, our passport photographs might just be copied and scanned and we wouldn't have a clue. Now, I would be the first to admit that I am more paranoid than Emmanuel Petit, and there are many who believe that having your details taken should only bother you if you expect to be doing something wrong in the future. But past experience tells me better. A few years back I brought a copy of a certain daily newspaper only to find my face staring straight back at me. The photo was under a banner-heading asking the country if they could identify not only my ugly mug but also twelve or so others wanted by the police for starting a riot in central London. The thing was that the riot in question had taken place only the day before and, as I was actually travelling back to my Hertfordshire home from the island of Iona in Scotland at the time of my reading the article, my presence at that riot would have been virtually impossible. Iona is a small, very isolated island that lies of the western edge of Mull and is where I had spent the previous nine weeks working as a volunteer at a Christian Abbey! The Old Bill had their reasons for putting my mug in the paper, I know, but that's an entirely different story – my point here being that once they get their nails into you they don't let go. However, they would have struggled to get a conviction on that one, what with 200 Christians and a couple of vicars in the dock to back me up. Nonetheless there I was, a lesson that being a little paranoid can be good for your soul.

Back at Harwich an officer would reappear every few minutes from the back office and begin calling out the names of those being given clearance to board the ferry, one of which brings a little light relief: 'Mr Holland?'

As he heads off a loud chorus follows his footsteps. 'Who are ya? Who are ya?'

It's funny to observe that prior to getting their passport back, every lad is doing his best to look angelic and a little disinterested, and yet the second that little book is placed back in their mitt they head off up the ramp giving it the old Liam large one. As Keef and I finally set foot on the boat we are greeted by one last copper, this time of the Dutch variety asking the most dumb question yet: 'Are you gentlemen intending to start fighting on the boat or will you be behaving yourselves today?'

What does he expect us to say? 'Well, we were thinking of having a few pints first then perhaps kicking it off once we were halfway across. Why, is that going to prove a problem, officer?' Once on board we head for the bar along with just about everyone else and toast the fact that in less than seven hours time we shall find ourselves safely ensconced in the Dutch capital.

With little else to do but drink, we decide to take a breather from the alcohol and head off for a wander around the deck. As we go we share stories of getting stoned, throwing up and personal sexual conquests, during which I find that Keef has discovered more uses for a cucumber than Delia Smith could ever possibly dream of. When walking around we bump into a group of lads, some of whom are wearing Ipswich Town shirts while one is sporting the yellow of their bitter rivals Norwich City! They offer the feeble excuse for travelling together, that of living in Lowestoft, a nowhere town the population of which is apparently split between yellow and blue! They tell me this obviously thinking that for some reason I might actually be interested, like I might actually care what goes on out in baby-eating country. Once I return from my coma, however, I find out that I do have a connection with one of the group after all. He's a lad called Daryl whose best mate appeared on the front cover of the book I wrote about France '98, *Tear Gas and Ticket Touts*. In the picture Daryl's mate is surrounded by tear-gas smoke and is kicking away the canister that had been fired towards him by the French riot police; he loves the picture because it totally captures the mood of events involving the England fans down in Marseille, and he has a blown-up copy hanging proudly on his wall just to remind him of what it was like. Daryl then goes on to tell me something I found rather interesting. Apparently, he likes a lot of the stuff I post on the Internet – which is curious because up until a month ago I had never even been on the Internet, computers having always scared the shit out of me. He tells me of a site called soccer-hooligan.com where someone is obviously posting stuff under my name! Wow, what a loser that bloke must be – surely if you have something to say you might as well say it yourself. So, mate, get a life will ya!

It turns out that Daryl's life is more desperate than I thought: as well as being a season-ticket holder at Portman Road, he works as an actor – an actor currently earning his corn performing in that standard summer play *Scrooge*. See, I told you – Lowestoft, a town with its finger right on the pulse! Another lad in their party is Steve, one of three Rushden and Diamonds fans making up their number. Steve tells me that just three days earlier he had been involved in a HGV accident. Now I am thinking: how unlucky can this group of lads get! Ipswich, Norwich, *Scrooge*, motorway pile-ups, etc. . . . Steve's back is covered in stitches, but fair play to him: despite the pain he had insisted on making the trip because of his love for England and the national football team. Well, one out of five ain't that bad, I suppose. Not for that neck of the woods, anyway. They are a good bunch of lads but before their bad luck rubs off on Keef and me, and the ferry starts sinking, we feel it best we move off and get back on the lager.

Playing on the television screens is the opening match for the Turks, who are taking on the Italians. Looking at the crowd you'd think the match was being played in Istanbul rather than Arnhem, Holland, but it seems Italy can count on the added support of just about every Englishmen on this ferry. When ordering more beer, Keef arrives at the conclusion that all Dutch people must have mastered their English accent while watching old Sean Connery 007 movies. Every one of them slurs their S's and adds an H to certain words; 'Yoush wanting two lagersh, yesh? Or maybe shome sexshy, sexshy ladiesh?' This is a discovery that has us in stitches now and will stick with us for the rest of the trip, much to the annoyance of the barman who by now doesn't even ask our order – instead, he just pours.

Because of the ferry's late departure we miss our connecting train to Amsterdam and are forced into making a much slower journey. During the trip I meet a Spurs fan who tells me his mate got done for indecent exposure at Vicarage Road (something that doesn't surprise me, as the Watford Old Bill are always on the lookout for cocks because they are well known as a bunch of twats). We also witness a lad from Lancashire having one of his eyebrows shaved off. When he wakes he is more than a little unhappy and spends the rest of the journey reminding his mates in no uncertain terms that sooner or later they will have to sleep themselves and then he will have his razor at the ready.

We eventually arrive in the Dam at just after six o'clock and quickly head off in search of a room for the night. Milling around outside the station are hundreds of lads looking just as lost, but none of the usual hotel touts you expect to find outside the capital's Central Station. Being the international traveller that I am, I convince Keef to follow me and proceed to lead him away from the throng as well as away from all the hotels. We spend the next half-hour wandering aimlessly up side-streets and weighing up the pros and cons of sleeping rough in one of the many empty barges lining the canals. We agree that if we have no luck, we'll spend the money we save either on getting so drunk that we'll just fall over and won't care where we sleep, or on trying to find some speed to keep us awake – and enable us to drink more!

Eventually we find a hotel not bearing the sign 'SORRY, FULL' and decide to give it a go. Keef reckons the place looks really expensive and well out of our reach, but it turns out to be £32 each and basically shit, so we take it! Staying in the same place are a few Birmingham fans and an Albion lad who tell us that in the battle of the takeaways the pizza-boys dicked the kebab-burners 2–1 thanks to a very dubious penalty – lovely, couldn't have happened to a nicer bunch. They also tell us that the game was held up for a while when some Turkish supporters started throwing bottles and air horns on to the pitch, something that was later to land the Turks with a £4000 fine. We find a bar just in time to catch the last knockings of France v. Denmark, a game more one-sided than Gary Neville's passing ability. The Danes are poor and Peter Schmeichel looks a shadow of his former self.

Being in Amsterdam to see the Dutch play their opening match was something I had been looking forward to for weeks. I love the Dutch; they're absolutely mad people, the Aussies of Europe. Nothing seems more important than just having a good time and, as expected, the locals were really up for it. Every bar was awash with the traditional Dutch Orange. Clog-hats, wigs, dyed hair and face-paint. OK, so they look like a bunch of twats, but they're Dutch so you kind of expect it. When the English do all that shit it's kind of different. We look like cunts rather than twats, you know what I mean? There's a difference. The Dutch appear to be taking the piss, whereas whenever you see a bloke walking down Wembley Way in his dyed wig he looks like he actually means it, like it's some kind of 'I am really wacky, me' statement, when the truth is 'No, you're not, mate, you're just a wanker in a wig'.

We enter a bar that's crammed with young Dutchski blokes and very horny, sexshe young Dutch girlsh. As least if the footy's shite we can stare at the crumpet. We move to the back of the bar where suddenly the Orange wigs and stuff stop and a line of lads in designer clothing begins, Ah, English, I presume! We begin talking to a lad from Kettering who, like so many others, is travelling alone. He is a member of the Official Travel Club and has a ticket for the match tomorrow, but has unfortunately lost most of his money and is out mine-sweeping the bars in the hope of getting pissed before going off to do a bit of window-shopping in the red-light district. After a few minutes we find out he's a follower of Tottenham, and when I ask him how he felt Spurs had done during the previous season he became rather annoyed:

> I haven't set foot in White Hart Lane since that bastard took over as manager. I can't believe what they have done to us at Spurs. Sugar should be fucking ashamed of himself. And I can't believe that so many Spurs fans put up with it. George Graham is scum, through and through – he even admits he still supports Arsenal, for fuck's sake! If any other Arsenal fan sat down at White Hart Lane on a Saturday and admitted to supporting them he'd get a right hiding, and yet they let him sit in the fucking dug-out. The best bit of news I had last year was when I heard he'd gone into hospital. I thought, 'Thank fuck for that, I can start going again soon!' Arsenal fans laugh at Spurs because of that bastard, they piss themselves. It's a bloody disgrace! I want to go back and as soon as he's gone I'll go back like a shot, but not while he's there, no way. I save my money now and watch England. I've always followed England anyway. The thing is, I'll always be Spurs through and through; I can't change that and that's why it hurts so much. Imagine your lot being managed by David Pleat!

That last comment has me choking on my lager, so at half-time Keef and I decide to head off to find another bar. As we spill out on to the street we notice that the bar opposite is exclusively full of English, many of whom are out on the street singing and looking pretty pissed. The bar is called The Grasshopper, and keeping a watchful eye on proceedings are two carefully positioned vanloads of Dutch police. Keef and I move on, thinking it's better to steer clear if we want to watch the second half of the match. After walking a few hundred yards we find ourselves on the main drag, standing outside a bar called Teasers. Inside there appears to be a full-on hardcore disco taking place. I can't help but notice that prancing around in the window for all his worth is a Jock wearing a floppy hat, a flag around his neck and a kilt. The place is jumping and so we decide to go in and join the party. Loudly banging out is the most annoying Euro-hardcore-uplifting-smurf pop you could ever have the misfortune to hear, which has me thinking there's no way I'm staying in here for forty-five minutes. I go to leave but Keef grabs my arm and draws my attention towards the bar. Standing atop the serving counter is a girl of Olympic proportions. An Asian babe, with legs up to the ceiling and a face that would have even Dale Winton thinking of things that don't come naturally to him. She has a figure to die for, is wearing a bright-orange thong and a tight fitting T-shirt. Keef orders two pints and we sit back to enjoy the view . . . er, sorry, the second half. The rest of the girls working the bar are of the same standard, each one completely gorgeous. Collectively, one of their most endearing features is the fact that they spend as much time eyeing themselves up in the mirror as we do gawping at them from a distance. It's something that Keef and I are agreeing is very, very sexshe indeed, yesh.

Unfortunately our second-half viewing is spoiled by the odd piece of exciting play on the pitch. The Dutch, most people's pre-tournament favourites, are slowly but surely finding themselves outplayed by a Czech side high on skill and mighty on defensive teamwork. As the home fans become a little quiet a few Norwegian lads start singing away, a rattle which is thankfully drowned out by a quick blast of the techno version of the *Blankety Blank* theme tune, a tune that sends the place mental once again and brings the girls back on to the bar. This time, the Asian goddess pours two jugs of ice-cold water over her head, an action that as if by magic quietens the place down and produces two nipples the size of coat-hangers from the front of her soaking shirt. More beer please, bartender!

With seconds to go, the Dutch midfielder Ronald De Boer moves into the box before taking the kind of dive that begs the response 'Cheating Dutch bastard'. Amazingly the referee points to the spot. The Italian official in question is Mr Pierluigi Collina, a man who has the appearance of a burned tortoise out of his shell who's been caught in a car's headlights crossed with Uncle

Fester from the Addams Family, all wide-eyed, wrinkly and not really much of a catch. Many believe him to be the best referee in the world! But after watching the replay on the big screen, even the Dutch supporters in the bar begin to look embarrassed by the decision, while Keef is far from happy. Until this point he had wanted the Dutch to win; now all he wants is for the penalty to go high and wide. Unfortunately his hopes are dashed as Ronald De Boer's twin brother, Frank, slams the ball home and the place erupts. Not even the dancing girls can curb Keef's sense of injustice; 'Cheating cunts. I hate that.' He nods in the direction of our own personal Miss Asia, who is once again giving it large on the bar.

'I bet she's a lady-boy an' all. Cheating fuckers.' We drink up and leave.

At a press conference later, the Flying Dutchman that is Ronald De Boer openly admits to making the most of his fall. It amazes me how accepted such statements have become in the modern game. It's as if cheating now forms part of the training manual, is almost an art form in itself. Unfortunately, players appear to get away with such actions and statements, whereas the man who blows the whistle is sure to get nothing but grief.

Pretty soon Keef and I find ourselves smack bang in the middle of the city's famous red light district. There can be no doubt about it: some of these birds knocking it out for money really are the mutt's nuts, the kind of women who would turn most blokes' heads and make most women jealous. Why they choose to earn their living in such a way defies belief, although I expect given the choice most of them would rather be living a different life altogether. Still, who am I to be all moral? Here I am, looking as much of a perv as anyone else, wandering the canal towpaths, laughing at the butt-plugs, rubber fists and assorted implements. I tell you, some of that stuff makes my eyes water just looking at it. God knows what happens once you plug it in or pull the rip-cord!

There are surprisingly few Dutch fans out and about celebrating their 1–0 victory. Nearly everyone we see is either an

Englishmen on the piss or a Japanese businessman on the lookout for your more horizontal type of refreshment. On passing by a busy bar, I suddenly hear someone call out my name. It's my mate Don, an old schoolfriend from Hemel Hempstead and a fellow Hornet. Now Don is a right wind-up merchant, the kind of bloke who pushes it as far as he can go but then pulls it back round just before someone clouts him . . . Then he'll start again. Yes, everybody knows a bloke like Don. The thing that gets Don out of trouble is that he's a very funny bloke with it; if he weren't he'd probably be dead by now. He's also a big drinker, but tonight appears to be amazingly sober and is also looking more than a little concerned.

He tells us that a window has just been put through in the shop next door. Apparently some local guy, a street junkie who was getting pissed-off by the English taking the mickey out of him, had done the deed. Now, though, the Dutch feds were beginning to move in and the atmosphere was turning. Outside, the England fans were starting to sing for all their worth, their chorus echoed by those of us sitting safely inside the bar.

'Ing-ger-land, Ing-ger-land, Ing-ger-land . . .'

For me, there's nothing like the feeling of hearing that ring out late at night in a foreign city – lovely. But Don has had enough, so he and a couple of others decide to move off to a bar a few doors down the street. As we finish our beers, we begin talking to a young Leeds fan who tells us of a rumour going around about a few English lads having a knife pulled on them by some Dutch fans out looking for a fight just around the corner from the bar. On seeing the knife the English lads had been on their toes and running for their lives, which to me and Keef seemed the best option – well, wouldn't you? Then Keef comes back from the bar empty-handed, telling me that the barmaid has been told by the police to close the place down. We get out as quick as possible. I don't know about you, but I find it's never good to be the last one in a bar the police are trying to clear – especially when you happen to be an English football fan on foreign soil. Like Don, we head away from where the police are flexing their muscles and head off into the night. At each bridge the words coca, puff, ecstasy and charlie cut through the general background noise as the local pushers go about their business. Having the English in town obviously isn't good news for the drugs trade, however: all we want to do is drink.

Now that we are even more pissed we spend even more time gawping at the whores, dribbling like a bunch of retards. I swear, you can almost see the pervy little thought-bubbles popping above our heads as we stumble from window to window.

We find ourselves stopping outside one particular building that plays host to five different women. Keef is convinced that not all is quite what it should be – he proceeds to ask passers-by if they think the girls in the window are actually boys, and very quickly a crowd of some ten to fifteen English football fans are considering the matter. Then a bloke walks up and knocks on the door. The perv is obviously in the mood for some serious action and quickly starts bartering with one of the tarts. Suddenly, though, he turns to leave, looking slightly frustrated. Keef yells after him; 'Oi, mate, can I ask you something?' The man stops.

'Yesh, shure. What is it you are wanting to know?'

'Are they birds or blokes in there?'

'Ah, dhis here ish a lady-boysh housh. But I am thinking a little too expenshive.'

A collective 'Uurrrhhhh' rings out from the gathered crowd and we move away as one from the local sex-case and scuttle off into the night. Eventually we stumble our way back to the bar that had earlier been closed down, only to discover that police have now closed the bridge off and are refusing to let anyone else enter the area. From behind the police line we can see and hear an English mob giving it all they've got, but with absolutely no chance of joining them we stagger back towards our hotel and kiss the city goodnight. Christ, following England doesn't half give you some memories!

11

Who's the Poor Bastard
in the Black?

The penalty decision leading to Holland's victory had disgusted Keef, and it also had us contemplating why anyone in their right mind would want to be a referee in this day and age. However, the world of football throws up some weird and wonderful moments, one of which occurred during a friendly match between Macau and Hong Kong just a few weeks before the start of Euro 2000. The incident centred on match-referee Mr Choi Kuok-Kun and the Hong Kong winger Lee Kin-Wo. Kin-Wo had just been sent off and referee Kuok-Kun was busy sorting out the usual moaning and verbal when Kin-Wo suddenly turned and booted the ball directly at him. Never again could the winger be accused by his teammates of failing to hit a barn door let alone a referee from ten paces, because this volley scored a direct hit. For a split second the referee appeared stunned by Kin-Wo's descent, then something apparently clicked in his mind – for he suddenly lost all self-control, steamed forward and planted the player a firm right-hander: bosh!

Oh, yes, forget the violent content, forget any kind of moral high-ground – that was a pure golden moment. I can't believe for one moment that there is a single referee anywhere in the world who saw that incident and didn't allow him or herself a wry smile when Kuok-Kun's fist hit home. Just imagine if Premiership referee Andy D'Urso had done the same thing to Roy Keane and co. following those disgraceful scenes at Old Trafford Ah! Would that have been the dog's bollocks or what? Go on, admit it – it would have been fucking marvellous.

I love referee Choi Kuok-Kun. Not because his name reminds me of something I'd expect to see in a Thailand bar involving dancing girls and ping-pong balls, but because his punch represented a small amount of payback for referees everywhere. Payback at the end of a season when the task faced by the man in the middle was made almost unbearable by the actions of players, managers and the game's top bods. Like 99.999 per cent of football fans, I have done my fair share of referee-bashing. It is because of a referee that to this day I refuse to acknowledge that Liverpool won the Double in 1986. My stubbornness is in response to the worst dive and subsequent penalty decision I have ever seen: just three minutes from time in an FA Cup quarter-final replay at Vicarage Road, Ian Rush did a 5.9 triple-flip and conned the moron in black into pointing to the spot. At the time, Watford were winning 1–0 but from then on the game went tits up and the record-books show that Liverpool went on to win 3–1 in extra time. They then won their semi against Southampton and eventually lifted the cup – and all because of one decision. Bastards! I'll never accept that Double and it makes my blood boil just to think about it; but personal grievances aside, I now have to concede that following the 1999–2000 season, even I feel sorry for the man in the middle.

Week in, week out, referees' performances are scrutinised on television and ripped apart by pundits, players and managers. Every error made is highlighted, every mistake is pounced upon, slaughtered and slayed as all and sundry seek to pass the buck in the easiest way possible. The usual sound bites flow thick and fast as referees find themselves accused of costing players their livelihoods and careers or even the clubs their league status; and yet when players tumble, dive and blatantly con their way to victory the airwaves fall noticeably silent. For me one example of such double standards was when the Leeds

United player Harry Kewell 'won' that penalty at Derby County's Pride Park in the last minute in December 1999. Pick twelve good men and true and I am sure the decision would be unanimous: he dived. I know David O'Leary calls the current Leeds team his babies, but not even toddlers fall over that much. He dived, blatantly – you know it, I know it – but did anyone on television have the bollocks to really pull him up? Did they fuck! Wouldn't it have been lovely to hear Trevor Brooking just once telling it like it is: 'Well you can't blame the ref – Harry Kewell fucking dived, the tosser.' You have to admit that would have been top TV. The unfortunate truth is that most Leeds fans don't give a monkey's, just like the rest of us don't when it goes our way. For them, Harry turned one point into three. However, if we are talking about people costing other players their livelihoods, their chance of survival or even a place in the Champions League, should we really be pointing only in the direction of the man in black? No. It's all too easy to blame the officials – the managers and players know that and as fans we buy it every time because, like them, we refuse to admit our team's own shortcomings.

The referee is faced with the unfortunate situation of being out there on his own. However, the greatest problem referees have to deal with is that deep down every football fan *thinks* they could have been a top player, whereas deep down every fan really *believes* themselves to be a top referee. And if you think the refs have it tough up in the Premiership, then just imagine what it must be like for the poor sod who gets up on a Sunday morning and has to cope with the likes of you and me. One such person is Ref X, whose personal account might just put you off had you ever considered taking up the whistle.

Sunday mornings are the worst, purely because the Saturday lads are usually of a higher standard and take their football that bit more seriously. On Sundays you get lads who are still pissed, still spaced-out, and the vast majority of them are useless. There has been many a time I've woken up on a Sunday, looked out at the rain and then remembered who I was actually refereeing that morning and thought to myself, 'Sod this for a game of soldiers'.

Some weeks it's like Beirut. In the six years I've been refereeing, I've been punched and kicked, I've been spat at, on more than one occasion I've been threatened with a good kicking in the showers after the game, and I've had my car surrounded in the carpark and booted as I've driven off. It can be really frightening, and when you take into account that I am still relatively young and fit it makes you wonder – maybe some blokes see that as a challenge, I don't know. But it's no wonder they struggle to get new lads in to do the job. Believe me, there are times when it's really not much fun. And when I watch some of the old boys taking the amount of stick they get, I can't help but think I'll pack up before I get that much older. Some of those old boys must be either bullet-proof, living a death-wish or just plain stupid. I've seen some terrible intimidation of older referees by young lads, blokes who think they're hard because they scare some poor old boy. It's sickening. I think a lot of the time the lads just totally lose control. If they could actually see themselves I think most of them would be really ashamed of how they behaved. But I've had my fair share of that as well, and there are certainly pubs in my town I wouldn't go near for fear of getting beaten up.

Many times things get so out of hand on the pitch between the teams you think, 'Bollocks to this' – but, of course, who gets it? Yours truly. A lot of the time you end up in a no-win situation and suddenly you're right in it. One team thinks you've bottled it and the other thinks you're a soft touch. That's the one thing I really hate; getting accused of bottling out. It's such an easy excuse for a team to throw and it then makes it so much harder for you to get any control back. I hate that, especially when you've actually tried to calm things down by giving a couple of cards and they just have no effect whatsoever.

You think, 'Hang on, this team are obviously a bunch of meatheads and they don't give a toss. Now there are eleven players on the other team and just one of me and yet they want me to put my head on the line and sort them out! Yeah, well, sod that. I've got a job to go to in the morning too and, like you, I want to go in one piece if that's at all possible.'

I hate to admit it, but there have been times when I've decided to look after number one first and foremost. I've not given penalties that I should have; I've not sent players off for tackles that should have seen them banned for life let alone taking an early shower; and I've given goals that were clearly offside for fear of getting my head kicked in by the team or their meathead fans on the line. I think any Sunday morning ref who tells you any different is either lying or in hospital. Trouble is that you then run the risk of getting a low score on the match-report sheet from the team you pissed off most, and that means going up before the ref's committee and having to explain yourself. That puts you in a difficult position, because if you have failed to book players or send them off you can't really tell the committee that you bottled out of doing so because you didn't want your head smashed in. Although that may be true, it doesn't really do you any favours with the committee and it stops you getting promoted because they mark you down as not being strong enough! It's a catch-22 situation because at the same time the violent teams get away with it because there are no sending offs or bookings against their name. Of course, all the referees talk and we all know who the bad teams are, but unless we all agree to stand up to them, they get away with it. Every now and again we can ask for an assessor to go and watch them, and fair enough they do act and ban teams if they catch them on a bad day. But nine times out of ten the teams know who the assessors are and once they spot them . . . well, surprise, surprise, they play like a bunch of choirboys.

They often lose, but at least they behave themselves.

The other thing that always gets me is when you have just suffered ninety minutes of abuse, been called everything under the sun, and once the game is over the players you've booked come over and are as nice as pie: 'Oh, you're not going to put that booking in are you, ref? It was just heat-of-the-moment stuff, you know how it is – sorry.' Yeah well, sod you. If I've been brave enough to book you then you must have really deserved it, pal. Believe me.

Then you get the kids' leagues. Wow, that's a whole different world, that is. These used to be the games that were fun to referee, but at times they get more out of hand than the blokes. Some of the kids have got no respect at all. They see *Match of the Day* and professional players chasing referees and they think that's how the game is played. Seeing the top players acting like that really does have an effect on the kids. They keep going on about being role models but continue to act like idiots. I would love some of them to come and see what effect they have on the kids – I am sure it would shock them. Every now and again, though, it does throw up some funny moments. I once had this Under-13s game to referee and this one kid was really mouthing off at me, I mean *really* mouthing off. I warned him and then had a word with his manager because he was starting to argue every throw-in, free-kick, everything. Then I gave this nothing free-kick and he blew. He was so angry he went as red as a beetroot. He came marching towards me, then he said: 'You're fucking crap, ref.' It was really funny, him trying to be all hard with his little high-pitched squeak, but that was it – I pulled him up, bent down and said: 'Oh, I am "fucking crap", am I? Well, you go and tell that to the shower, son, because I am sending you off for foul and abusive language. Bye-bye.'

You should have seen his face. The old bottom lip started twitching, then the eyes welled up. 'Please don't send me off, mister, please. If my mum finds out I swear she'll kill me. Please.'

'Yeah well, you should have thought of that beforehand, sonny – bye.' A little pat on the head and off he went with some of the other kids taking the piss because he was crying. That will probably scar him for life and he'll probably have a deep-rooted hatred for referees and anything official. Still, never mind . . .

That actually leads on to the next problem; the parents. Honestly, if you have never watched kids' football on a Sunday morning then I urge you to go. You have to see it to believe it. No wonder some kids turn out the way they do. The amount of pressure some of the parents put on their kids is unbelievable, frightening at times. At that level it should be just a game, but some dads place so much importance on it. The language and comments you get are unbelievable at times. I've had blokes shouting at me, 'You useless cunt, ref' at the top of their voices. Always a nice turn of phrase to use in front of the kids, I think, that one! I've heard people walking back to the car going, 'You were useless, son, shit. You'll never make a player as long as you've got a hole in your arse. I never thought a son of mine could be that crap at football.' And the kid's only eleven, for Christ's sake, give him a break. Of course, for some of the dads it really isn't their kids playing – it's them. They kick every ball, make every tackle and argue every decision. It's really difficult to deal with because what can you do? I can't actually send *them* off or ask *them* to leave, can I? And if you ask them to calm down they can turn really nasty – I mean, who wants to be told off in front of their kids. I've actually been quite lucky, but attacks on referees by dads watching their kids play are nothing new.

So, you might ask, why do I continue to do it? Well, it's simple: I love the game, I really do. I've never really been much of a team-player but I love football. For all I've said about the grief and abuse, I have to say that for every one bad match you get six or seven good ones. Tell someone you're a referee and they think one of three things: you're either mad; you have no friends; or you're some sort of little Hitler looking for a power-kick. Well, I like to think I fit into none of those categories, especially the last one – although I suppose you'd expect me to say that, really, wouldn't you? No, I do it because I love it. I certainly don't get a kick out of dishing out the cards or sending people off; that's not what the game's about. Players don't turn up on a Sunday to act like idiots on purpose. All eleven want to stay on the pitch, really – let's face it, your average Sunday player doesn't need the fine or the ban and I don't need the paperwork. I have to say, though, that getting up on a Sunday is getting tougher every season, because the job isn't getting any easier, and if I could knock it on the head I probably would. Saturdays are OK, but it's watching and refereeing the kids' games that really make it all worth it. Looking out for the kids who might just go on to do something – that's what's really rewarding and believe me, the skill-level that some of the youngsters show nowadays is unbelievable at times. I do like to think that I play a part in helping the game develop at that level as well, and that is really satisfying. If you get left alone to referee the kids properly you can really teach them the rules, and nine times out of ten they really respond and that is so important for the future of the game. It's just a shame that all the good work you put in often gets knocked out of them once winning becomes more important than enjoyment, and the trouble there is that winning is getting more important right down the age-groups.

The other big thing is the challenge. I really would like to referee at a higher level. There is always that next step up the ladder to aim for which makes it exciting, as I believe I can go a long way – much further than I could ever have dreamed of going as a player. Don't take that to mean I only took up refereeing because I was crap at football. I hate it when people say that. It is so patronising when you hear players and managers going on about referees not understanding the game. The truth is that the referee is a major part of the game. That is so often overlooked. Players need to understand that yes, being a referee is very different to being a player – as is the role of a goalkeeper compared to that of a centre-forward. Nonetheless we are an essential part of football. It would be just as easy for us to say that players don't understand the art of refereeing! Although I would definitely say that a lot of players don't fully understand the rules. Sorry, I had to get that one in, but unfortunately it's true. I think a lot of players and fans forget the simple fact that without the referee there simply wouldn't be a game at all.

It would appear that one of the major problems facing referees at the moment is a total lack of respect from both players and managers. Shameful images of referees being chased, abused and manhandled fill our television screens almost every week. Players hunting in packs like dogs after a piece of fresh meat, harangue, jostle and intimidate officials while using language that would, were the laws of the game strictly adhered to, lead to at least a booking if not an early dismissal. Managers now openly criticise the match-officials, even to the extent of asking for certain referees to be removed from their fixtures – something that disgracefully the FA have on occasion agreed to do, a fact both they and the clubs involved should be ashamed of. That quite unbelievable pandering to the top clubs has only fuelled the fire of those who delight in picking apart every mistake made by the people at the very centre of our game. It does nothing but strip the referees of their self-respect and add to the pressure of the job. And yet those very same managers continue to demonstrate a remarkable ability somehow to miss every foul word, exaggerated fall or elbow to the face that the cameras pick up involving their own playing-staff. So where did it all start to go wrong?

In terms of the English game, the turning-point surely occurred at Hillsborough in September 1998 when Paolo Di Canio, playing for Sheffield Wednesday against Arsenal, pushed referee Paul Alcock to the ground. Never before in this country had such an incident happened within football's topmost rank, and never before had the FA the chance to clamp down on what was already the major problem of player indiscipline. The initial reaction from the vast majority of supporters was that the Italian should be banned for life. There is no doubting Di Canio's ability; he is a truly remarkable player and his loss would have been a sad moment for the fans in this country. But his removal from the game was a necessary evil were the FA to be seen to be doing the right thing. The Italian brought shame on what was once considered the fairest and most honourable league in the world, and so should not have been allowed to kick a ball on these shores ever again. However, the FA once more demonstrated a lack of integrity and failed in their duty to maintain the right to protection offered to every referee in this country. While there is no doubt that banning Di Canio from the British game would render one of Sheffield Wednesday's then most expensive commodities suddenly worthless, surely here was an action that had to be taken. Even compensating the Yorkshire club for their loss would have been a small price to pay for sending out the starkest of messages to players and managers: place your hands on the referee and you are placing yourself in serious trouble. But no, despite the apparent backing of the player's club and his manager, the FA let a golden opportunity to tidy up the game slip through their fingers, a mistake that clearly went on to open a whole new can of worms.

The 1999–2000 season saw a major upturn in the amount of violent abuse directed towards referees by players at the top end of our domestic game. The directives continually given to referees during this time via the Football Association, UEFA and FIFA on how to handle player-abuse did little but force the officials further and further back into a corner from which there was often no escape. These instructions made U-turns that had referees clamping down (or, in other words, enforcing the rules) one minute and showing leniency the next. And all this at a time when their every move was being discussed, written about and assessed. Even Arsène Wenger admitted towards the end of the season that most clubs had taken advantage of the predicament our match officials had found themselves in! Yes, *Arsène Wenger!* Of course, the situation over here is as yet nowhere near as bad as it appears to be in many other countries. We have all seen images of referees being chased out of grounds in such places as South Africa and Argentina. During a World Cup qualifying match between Bolivia and Colombia in La Paz, the referee was head-butted by a player after the Colombian team captain was sent off – and that at a top international match! It sounds quite unbelievable, but just how long will it be before a top-flight referee finds himself on the end of a stiff right-hander from one of *our* top players? Some would argue that Di Canio's push should have been as close to such an incident as we'll ever see. Personally I very much doubt it will be.

To me, the argument that today's players are faster or harder than those of old and the modern referees are struggling to keep pace is pure drivel. In fact, I would argue that quite the opposite is true. Remember Chopper Harris, Billy Bremner and Graeme Souness? What I would give to see Souness tackle Vieira! That would give him something to moan about. Those old players were just as fast and were hard as hell, the difference being that yes, they would argue decisions. Yes, they would bawl at the referee if they were booked or sent off. But once the game restarted, either with or without them, everyone took it on board and got on with it. You never saw them in the papers the next day moaning like a bunch of twelve-year-olds. They never whinged about being a target for referees. You never heard them talk of packing it all in or going to play in another country where their 'talents' would be more appreciated. We all realise that just one bad decision can mean the difference between a step up the league ladder or yet another season with the also-rans – Redknapp, Fergie, Graham and co. remind us of this often enough. But so too can one glaring miss, one awful back-pass or a sending-off for petulantly kicking out at a player when a decision has already gone your way. Remember France '98, the Argies, Beckham? The stakes don't come much higher than a place in the quarter-finals of the World Cup, do they?

However, with the situation spiralling out of control, the Football Association have with their new directives at last set about placing their house in order, and for that I have nothing but praise. Their new disciplinary code of conduct should go a long way towards placing the control of the game back into the hands of the referee, and shows without doubt that after years in the doldrums English football still has the ability to take a lead within the world's game. Once bedded down, the strict penalties to be imposed on both players and managers who intimidate match officials should see a vast reduction in the ugly pitched battles that currently dog our domestic game. The possible deduction of points for those clubs who continually flout the new rules should see managers scouting not only for new talent but also for anger-management therapists in order to keep control of their star assets, while heavy fines and match bans should eventually curb even the most vocal players' tongues. Such measures will undoubtedly take time to take effect; managers will complain and some of our foreign imports will jump ship long before the dust settles. Nevertheless, if we ultimately find ourselves with a fairer contest, then all hail the FA for leading the way.

With so much at stake in the modern game, many are now asking for new technology to be brought in. They call for cameras in the goalposts, even in the ball! They want action-replays, a referee in each half, time-outs and such bollocks, all of which is great if you referee in the Premiership but little use if you happen to blow your whistle down at your local park. Personally I don't agree with using such technical advances, purely because it drives the sport even further away from those who take part in it at grass-roots level. As much as being a game of beautiful skill, football is also a game riddled with controversy. No amount of technology will ever change that. It always has been and always will. Referees mess up but so do players. (It doesn't matter how many cameras you have in the stand, Andy Cole will still miss nine or ten shockers in a season.) Let's stop trying to make the game foolproof. This growing desire to keep pace, move forward and embrace technology is stupid. Defeat is so rarely accepted with dignity within the modern game; there has to be an excuse for defeat other than referees being conned by players diving, faking injury or trying to get fellow professionals cautioned or sent from the field!

If the referees need help then give them it, but let's keep it simple. Surely we don't need an extra referee up in the stands when more of the decision-making could so easily be restored to those that run the line. I don't think a match goes by these days without me asking myself; 'Linesmen – what is the point?' For Christ's sake, give them something to do. There is nothing more infuriating than watching the ball go out of play just ten feet away from the guy holding the flag and then watching him wait for the referee to point the way of the throw-in. It drives me mental. As does watching them stand, holding their flag behind their back, whispering into the referee's ear like some naughty schoolkid grassing up his mate. It makes them look useless, without influence. Give them back some reason to exist, please. You never know – give them a bit of clout and it might even stop players hurling abuse their way every time a decision goes against them. Give the linesmen some real power, such as the authority to book players for mouthing, for elbows off the ball and for continual intimidation. In the build-up to Euro 2000, FIFA did take the positive step of rushing through legislation allowing the fourth official to draw the referee's attention to any off-the-ball incident occurring during a game. A positive step, yes, but let's go the whole hog if we really want to clamp down on the current aggressive attitude of players and managers. It's got to be worth a try.

With so much money flooding into the game it seems absolutely mad that one of the most influential men on the park is merely taking part in what amounts to nothing more than a paid hobby. Many argue against referees going full-time, suggesting that making them professional would have little if any effect on their ability to referee. What utter bollocks. Taking away the pressure of jostling work commitments with a refereeing schedule would *have* to prove beneficial. More time to train, to rest and to recover from injury would undoubtedly bring with it better fitness levels, thus making our referees sharper and keeping them closer to the action. The safety-net of a good wage would free up our top match-officials to go out into the schools and sports centres and educate young players in the rules of the game, providing the players of the future with greater understanding while simultaneously breaking down the barriers between players and officials. Towards the end of the 1999–2000 season, the FA announced that the fee for refereeing a Premiership match would rise from approximately £600 per match to £900, whereas lower down the ladder the fee would stabilise at a meagre £195. In a world where money rules, many of our referees are left looking like second-class citizens when the game should be acknowledging the reality of the major role they play and their place within football itself. By elevating the status of referees, by turning the task into a career rather than a hobby, we may well find that much-needed younger blood is drawn into the profession. We could well witness ex-players taking up the job – something many have for years wanted to see – although I do have my reservations about this: fans might react badly to the issue of perceived ex-club loyalties, and the amount of respect ex-player referees could hope to gain when dealing with former colleagues or even old friends is questionable.

Don't get me wrong: I am sure I still have many days left in me where I doubt the man in the middle's parenthood. And believe me when I say that in no way have I suddenly turned into some Draconian law lover harbouring a fetish for forty-year-old potbellied blokes with skin so pale you could watch slides on it. I am sure there are a few more dodgy decisions, missed elbows and wrongly disallowed goals to come that will have me denying results, debating in the pub and asking myself why I even bothered going to matches in the first place. But I do stop and ask myself this question: isn't that in many ways what football is about? Surely one of the game's greatest attractions is its element of what might have been, what should have been and the 'if only's. Just imagine how dull that post-match pint would become if every move had been scrutinised, sanitised and made perfect by invisible men watching an action replay up in the stands while the players stood around waiting. Try to imagine football without the debate, the disagreements and the controversy! I think they call it Gridiron in the good old US of A, and yes, it's shite, isn't it! It is easy to understand the frustration players and managers must feel when bad decisions go against them – easy because we, the fans, feel that frustration just as much. It drives us mad, has us jumping to our feet and bawling our heads off, but it ain't ever going to change the decision, is it!

As I've already said, I never in my life thought I would feel sorry for the bloke with the whistle, but I do. The poor old referee has been messed about for too long. A man alone being made a scapegoat for many of the game's problems. Their role has been overlooked and belittled, their importance drastically underestimated – so much so that they are often left to shoulder the responsibility and deal with the anger when teams fail to deliver. Well, I've had enough of seeing Ince and co. chasing referees. I no longer wish to see Arsène shifting the blame and I am sick of Sir Fergie defending a player's high tackle and suggesting that the victim, sprawled on the grass clutching his wedding tackle, is overacting. Order needs to be restored and the only way for that to happen is by giving the referee back first the control and subsequently the confidence he needs to officiate the game according to the rules. That way we might just see an end to incidents such as the one involving Di Canio and Alcock. For the time being, at least.

Before I leave the subject I must add that I asked my mate Ref X about his reaction to the punch delivered by referee Choi Kuok-Kun. His reply: 'Oh yes. That was top, that was. How many times do you think I've wanted to do that?'

Shame the poor sod was banned for life . . .

12

Player Violence

As the celebrity status of today's football stars reaches unprecedented heights, many find their actions both on and off the pitch coming under increasing scrutiny. Whether they like it or not, their status undoubtedly makes them role models for all who pay homage. And though there are numerous people within the game who still consider football-associated violence to be more a problem of society than of the sport, I find it increasingly hard to draw a wedge between the aggressive and violent behaviour of our star players and the current upturn in hooliganism among the fans.

Playing the part of role model must prove a difficult task, especially when the fact that many of our top star players are themselves very young and relatively inexperienced is taken into account. However, such inexperience coupled with the large disposable income many of these players now command can easily lead to some treading a most unfortunate path. Dealing with the actions of players when they are away from their clubs and living their personal lives obviously poses a problem for their employers, but it provides an opportunity for those at Lancaster Gate to send out a clear message – and to their credit the Football Association have not been slow in coming forward and attempting to raise standards. The FA moved swiftly when the two Leeds United stars Lee Bowyer and Jonathan Woodgate were arrested following an alleged racist attack outside a nightclub during which an Asian youth was beaten unconscious and left with a fractured skull, a fractured cheekbone, a broken leg and shattered ribs. Both players were immediately banned from playing for their country until after the court case had taken place, a decision that not only gave them clear indication of the consequences such allegations carry but also cost them their places in the England Under-21s Euro finals squad travelling to Slovenia. Chelsea's young star Jody Morris suffered the same ban following an incident resulting in a charge of actual bodily harm being laid against him. Once again the FA and the Under-21 team manager, Howard Wilkinson, clamped down hard in order to deflect any adverse publicity away from the national side. This was a brave move that in the long-term should benefit not only individual players, but also the England squad as a whole, and one for which the FA should be given well-earned praise.

At club level, however, the response to such discipline is often very different, as clubs pamper their assets, wrapping them in cotton-wool and defending them to the last in the hope of clinging on to what is, after all, a valuable commodity. When the Derby County player Marvin Robinson was jailed for head-butting a teenage girl (think about that charge for a second), the club reportedly made a statement claiming they felt the player had been harshly dealt with. This same statement also brought into question whether or not the court had decided to make an example of their player because of his professional status, a suggestion that is not only insulting to the victim of the attack, but which also sends out all the wrong signals to the youngsters that look up to their footballing heroes. At a time when many footballers, managers and club chairmen appear to want to have their cake and eat it, the level of violence on the pitch between certain so-called professionals has reached an all-time high as mass-brawls, in-fighting and off-the-ball incidents occur with ever-increasing regularity.

The level of brutality raging out on the pitch recently between players of Wolverhampton Wanderers and Nottingham Forest led to police taking the unprecedented step of entering both teams' dressing-rooms at half-time and stating that they were prepared to use their powers of arrest if those involved did not curb their aggression and get on with the game. Up until this time it had often been assumed that footballers and the game's authorities think themselves above the law, but the police action taken at Molineux demonstrated that patience with any such attitude had begun to run dry.

Of course, the major fear for the police is that incidents of on-field violence lead to problems in the stands as fans react to and imitate those representing their team on the pitch. The link is undeniable – acrimonious confrontations on the pitch *do* often result in discontent among the crowd – and yet managers defend their aggressive players to the end while referring to any volatile fan as mere pond life. The majority of managers, just like supporters, claim to be sickened by the hooligans' actions but apparently neglect to exert any real control over their own star men. Some choose to hide behind the pathetic excuse that aggression is just part of certain players' make-up, an ingredient without which they wouldn't be the same player. This is quite definitely bollocks, for as far as I know throwing punches off the ball and elbowing people in the face have never been within the rules of football!

Just a few weeks after their clash with Forest, Wolverhampton Wanderers once again found themselves in confrontation both on and off the pitch when they paid a visit to local rivals Birmingham City. Tension within the stadium was already at boiling-point – prior to kick-off more than 100 fans had clashed in what police described as a major disturbance – and yet despite the obvious need for everyone to keep a calm head on them, police were forced to enter the team dug-outs in order to defuse a heated exchange between the managers and coaching staff from both sides. During the match three players were given their marching orders as ill feeling led to violent conduct and allegations of cheating between players. (The most vocal of these came from City player Martin Grainger who, via the national press, later called one Wolves rival 'the most hated man in football'! Deserved or not, the tag will follow the player in question on to the pitch whenever he turns out to play against BCFC and faces their passionate supporters.) The violence on the pitch had those in the stands reaching boiling-point once again as throughout the match City fans showered their Midlands rivals with coins and missiles.

The reputation players build for themselves, whether or not deserved, among certain groups of fans often stays with them for the duration of their career, no matter what team they end up representing. In the current high-pressure world of professional football this has begun to pose a new problem, with players being seen openly clashing with those who pay to watch them. The final two months of the 1999–2000 season provided much evidence of such conflict. The first attack involved the Stoke City goalkeeper Gavin Ward and came after some fans alleged he made obscene hand-gestures towards supporters in the home end of Bristol Rovers Memorial Ground. Two fans stormed the pitch and began throwing punches at the keeper before police and stewards intervened, the Stoke manager later claiming the attack should have seen his team being awarded all three points. Just days later a similar incident occurred up at Darlington when, following a late equaliser by the home side, fans invaded the pitch – some of whom began attacking the Shrewsbury Town keeper Paul Edwards. At least one other player was said to have been kicked but, wary of controversy, the Shrews' then manager, Kevin Ratcliffe, would say only this: 'I did see something but it's not anything I want to comment on, and I'm sure Darlington don't want to either.' A bury-your-head-in-the-sand comment that provides little if any assistance to those trying to clean up the game. Following such a statement it was rather ironic that the next player to come under attack was Darlo's main striker at the time, Marco Gabbiadini, who was punched in the face by a fan as he left the pitch at local rivals Hartlepool. The Quakers' manager David Hodgson this time did *his* best to play down the incident, instructing Labbiadini not to take the matter any further. Hodgson also claimed to be have been hit by a 50p piece thrown from the crowd. His comment: 'Fans do that.' Oh, that's OK then.

The mass field-brawls and disputes involving top clubs such as Manchester United, Chelsea, Arsenal, Leeds, Tottenham, Middlesbrough, West Ham et al undoubtedly leave their mark. For those who spend their time working at grass-roots level this provides countless problems, and it's people such as Gary B. who often end up having to sort out the boys from the copycats:

There is no doubt about it: the kids imitate what they see on the telly. If you don't believe that then you should get down to the park on a Sunday and see it for yourself. Every Saturday I watch *Match of the Day* almost praying nothing terrible happens on the pitch because I know if it does I'll have my work cut out with the boys in the morning. Sometimes it's like starting all over again as you find yourself trying to tell them what's right and what's wrong. You see, they love football so much at that age and they are so impressionable, but unfortunately it's not just the good stuff they copy. I know many professional footballers do an awful lot of good work within schools and out in the community so I don't want to knock them too much, but sometimes I wish they could see the effect all the swearing and fighting has on the kids. Footballers are role models; you only have to look at the names on the back of the kids' shirts to see that. Come down our local park and I'll show you a dozen kids wearing a Manchester United shirt with 'Beckham' emblazoned across the back – they dream of being like him, they copy his every kick and every gesture and who can blame them? When he's behaving, the lad's a genius.

But for me there is nothing more depressing than seeing a whole bunch of ten-year-olds chasing after each other and swearing; it really saddens me but I've seen it so many times now and it is becoming more commonplace. Little kids punching and screaming at each other when at that age they should be just having fun and learning the basics of the game without any pressure. Of course, it's important to instil a competitive nature, but at that age it isn't everything – learning the basic skills, passing, tackling, heading, and teaching them to respect the ref and play by the rules are far more important. At our club we are trying really hard; we have to. We've put into place a code among the coaches where we will take a lad off or not play them at all if they act up too much. Swearing is a big no-no within our set-up – that's the one we are really trying to stamp out. That and answering back to the referee. If they argue with the ref they know they'll get a warning from the side-line straight away, and if they do it again that's it: they're taken off. Nothing to do with the ref, it's our decision. Of course, the referees like that because it takes the pressure off them. It seems to be working well, because all the kids really want to do is play football and this teaches them they can't do that from the side of the pitch or when they're sulking in the car because they've been substituted. Of course, the problem comes when they move up through the age-groups and it does become more about the winning than just having fun. I only hope that what we're teaching them now will stick with them when they're older, so that if any of them do make the big time they'll be the ones clever enough to stand back and watch when all the others are trying to beat the living daylights out of each other. It's just a shame they didn't teach some of our current pros the same lessons when they were first kicking a ball about!

Once again the position of players as role models for kids is brought into question. After all, it is the children who have the future of the sport at their feet, a fact the FA have been quick to acknowledge – and with aggressive behaviour among our current professionals spiralling out of control, they were forced into action. The fact that Manchester United captain Roy Keane received the Footballer of the Year award in a season when allegations were laid against him about his conduct both on and off the field certainly implies that many now see aggressive behaviour as part and parcel of the game.

The measures brought in by the FA at the start of the 2000–01 season suggest in no uncertain terms that the time has come for players and managers to clean up their act. Heavy fines for continual poor discipline, lengthy bans for players and managers who intimidate referees, and the introduction of a video-review panel to clamp down on off-the-ball incidents such as spitting and the elbowing of opponents are all major steps forward in turning the English domestic league into not only the best but also the fairest set-up of its kind in the world. However, the threat introduced and standing head and shoulders above the rest is the possibility of a deduction of league points for offences committed. This is a long overdue measure that should send shockwaves around boardrooms and clean up the game almost overnight as players and managers suddenly wake up to the reality that excuses and self-pity offer little comfort to shareholders interested purely in a return on their dividends. A shove on the referee's chest could now mean the difference between promotion, relegation or even – God forbid – a place in the Champions League rather than just the transfer from the club of the player concerned, surely a positive move forward in the race to rid the game of such cowardly intimidation.

If the sickening Di Canio incident marked a turning-point in English football and demonstrated that discipline among players had reached an all-time low, the FA's failure to ban him from the British game for life was not only an insult to all referees but also to all true sportsmen and women throughout the country. However, now those at headquarter have finally stamped their authority on the sport, we must surely stand and applaud their actions. By introducing such fierce punishments, the FA have firmly planted the ball in the clubs' penalty area; now all that remains to be seen is whether or not those clubs do a Philip Neville and slide themselves into deeper trouble.

13

Shattered Dreams and the Straining of Greens

Monday 12 June 2000

The long-awaited day has finally arrived for the England team to kick-off their Euro 2000 campaign, and so the main task ahead for Keef and me is that of hunting down a couple of match tickets. Experience tells me that it is always best to leave ticket-hunting until the last possible minute. Only a Muppet would buy a ticket weeks in advance, as you're guaranteed to be paying way over the odds even by the touts' standards. I've never been one for paying hundreds of pounds for tickets anyway; the highest I've ever forked out being £125 to see England play Romania during France 98. (A match we lost 2–1!) I've never understood why someone would pay four to five hundred quid to see one match. The price of a season ticket wasted on just ninety minutes? No way! You must be mad. I've never in my life seen a match worth that kind of money. For £500 I'd expect to play myself before getting brought off by Melinda Messenger at half-time.

While we're eating that outstanding continental breakfast of dry bread, jam and more dry bread, the television brings the good news that the streets of Holland have remained trouble-free as far as English fans are concerned. The item helps to make talking to the waiter a little less embarrassing, so we ask him whether or not he can point us in the direction of any match tickets. He tells us to try the newsagents on the corner. However, less than twenty minutes later his quite convincing suggestion appears to have been either a red herring or a top method for getting the gassy pair of us out of his dining room before one of the other punters keels over and dies. On leaving the hotel we bump into the lads from Birmingham again who tell us that late on last night things got a little heated with the Old Bill up by the bridge. Apparently they got slightly narked by the fact that the English lads wouldn't stop singing when they asked them to, so they dished out a few slaps with the old truncheons to quieten things down.

By ten o'clock Keef and I are once again wandering the streets aimlessly and winding our way back towards the red light district like two dogs sniffing out a bone. With little else to do, Keef is keen to see whether or not the ladies of the night are still at it and if they look as good in the daylight as they did the night before. As we pass one of the windows I spot an old boy of about eighty cleaning the floor with a bucket and mop.

'Fuck me,' I say. 'I know we were pissed but not *that* pissed, surely!'

'I don't know, take his teeth out and close your eyes and you wouldn't know the difference,' Keef replies, then adds, 'I wouldn't like to sniff that mop, though, would you?'

A few yards on we enter one of the area's many sex shops and after an initial fit of giggles start flicking through the masses of porn on offer. From the other side of the aisle, all I can hear are Keef's disgusted mutterings: 'Oh, for God's sake!'; 'Jesus, fuckin' no!'

The place is full of pure filth – everything you can think of as well as a few things you wouldn't have thought possible. Videos such as *Wives Over Sixty*, the cover of which shows an old granny looking like her body's been ironed by a drunk monkey! From across the shop Keef suddenly pipes up once more: 'Ah, now *that's* clever! Not nice, but clever.' I will not describe this video cover for fear of getting sued. However, to give you some idea of the suggested storyline I will say only this; remember the saying, 'You can't teach an old dog new tricks'? Well, believe me, that's bollocks! We then spot the video to top all videos, its title *Fucked by Fish*! On the cover is a bloke with a massive bone-on getting sucked off by a carp . . . and so we leave!

Once back in the real world we decide to head up to the station and start asking around for tickets. Almost immediately I hear the immortal words, 'Tickets! Buying or selling! Anyone need tickets?'

As ever, it's the same old faces doing the dealing. Whether it's football or rock concerts, in London, Liverpool or Amsterdam, you can always count on the same firm of lads turning up to offer you that golden ticket – but always at a price. The particular figure they have in mind this time is £200, way out of our reach. I had promised Keef before coming out to Holland that I would go to the game only if we could both go. Now we are both strapped for cash and have already spent a lot more on the hotel and beers than we had expected to. I have the luxury of knowing I'm coming out again anyway, as I'm going to try my luck at both the Germany and Romanian games, but for Keef this is it as far as Euro 2000 is concerned, so we've agreed that if we can't both get a ticket for less than £60 we'll stay in Amsterdam, get pissed, watch the game in a bar and then get pissed some more instead. And to be honest, I've always thought the chances of getting a ticket for £60 are virtually zero.

As we wander around the station we get talking to various lads making their way down to Eindhoven for the match. One lad supplies the information that if you have a valid match ticket then your train journey is given to you free, a nice touch but a little irrelevant as I hadn't intended to pay for a train ticket anyway. One of the touts then approaches us and asks how much we're prepared to hand over for a ticket, then offers one up at £100! Suddenly the old alarm bells start ringing out a happy tune. If I'd have been on my own I would have bitten his hand off at that price, but the amount of readies has halved in less than half an hour so I turn it down and suggest to Keef that we head off to a bar and sit tight for an hour or so. The fact that these lads are working up here in Amsterdam rather than down in Eindhoven suddenly has me thinking there must be a glut of tickets doing the rounds. If the tickets are fetching the kind of bread they're asking for, then why the hell are they making life difficult for themselves by being up here rather than where the majority of the ticketless England fans are sure to be? As we head off to the bar I begin to believe for the first time that Keef and I might just get to the match after all.

We park ourselves down at a bar on the main drag and watch in envy as hordes of English lads pass by on their way up to the station. As the hours tick by we begin to wonder whether or not a trip down to Eindhoven might prove a better option – at least that way we would get to see the game in a town full of Englishmen. But with rumours flying around the bar that the only beer on sale in Eindhoven is half-strength gnats' piss, Keef is easily swayed in favour of staying put, whereas I really want to be where the action is – after all, this is meant to be a football trip! Slowly but surely the touts are moving further and further away from the station in the hope of catching ticketless fans as early as possible and prise out an extra few shekels for their endeavours. I have convinced Keef to leave the bartering to me because I have *been there* and *done it all* before. I have also convinced him to let me work out the exchange-rate, as the touts want to deal in Dutch guilders rather than in pound notes. Suddenly a guy walks past and asks if anyone wants tickets – but once again the asking price is £100. Acting the cocky idiot, I pretend to be half interested but tell him to leave it as we'll get one at face-value down in Eindhoven. Off he goes only to return ten minutes later saying we can have two tickets for £75 each. So near and yet so far. In the best Del Boy manner I can muster I continue to act the goat: 'Sorry, mate. The best I'll give you is 500 guilders for the pair.'

'Fuck off, I'm not letting them go for that, mate, no way.' And with that off he trots once more to join his mates. I watch as the group of them begin to discuss my offer and then, with a bit of a swagger, I turn to Keef. 'He'll be back,' I say, and before Keef can reply the lad backs up my claim and returns with his mates. 'Told ya.'

'Five hundred guilders for two, yeah?'

'Yes mate, that's the best I'll go.'

'All right, then, 500 it is!' The lad's voice has an edge of surprise but I hand over the cash and off he goes. I couldn't believe it – there they were, two tickets sitting in my palm.

The feeling is tremendous. Having resigned myself to staying put I'm now suddenly chuffed beyond belief. The thought of seeing England play sends a rush through my veins and lifts me out of my seat. I give the tickets the once-over yet again, and find that not only are we going to the match but that the tickets we've just bought will have us sitting right next to each other. As Keef and I congratulate ourselves, one of the lads sitting on the next table pipes up: 'Ah, you lucky bastards, how much did you pay?'

'Five hundred guilders for the two.' I wave the tickets at his face.

'Five hundred? Fair play, mate. £150 – £75 each – not bad.' His reply suddenly stops the celebrations.

'No, what do you mean, £150? Five hundred guilders is £120 . . . isn't it?'

'No, it's £150.' Suddenly the penny drops.

'Ed, you dozy cunt!' was the best Keef could offer as the realisation hit that I hadn't worked out the correct exchange rate. No wonder the lad had come back so quick. He had offered me tickets at £75 and like a fool I had replied, 'No way, mate, but I'll give you £75.'

As we head off to the station I try to convince Keef that with saving on the train fare the money thing doesn't work out that badly, but he is having none of it and so I'm forced to concede that any further bartering will be left to him. Still, it's only money anyway; and within twenty minutes we're sitting on the train heading south out of Amsterdam Central towards Eindhoven.

* * *

As expected, the train is crammed with excited England fans and we soon find ourselves sitting next to Alan and Sally, a middle-aged couple from Suffolk. They both work for a Japanese bank based in London and are obviously football mad. Alan supports Man United while his wife – a right looker, it must be said – follows: 1) Ipswich, because she was brought up down that way; 2) Barnsley, because her father supported them; and finally 3) United because of hubby Alan! He supports them simply because in his opinion Ipswich are shit and, like most United fans you meet who live outside of Manchester, he also offers the excuse that he's followed the Reds since he was a kid! The Ipswich/Barnsley thing had apparently given Sally a right dilemma during the play-offs at Wembley just weeks before Euro 2000, but she'd ultimately decided she couldn't lose and so had just enjoyed the day for all she could. Oh, what it must be like to be that impartial! They have been saving up for this trip for more than three years and have already taken in three of the games: the opening-ceremony fixture between Belgium and Sweden in Brussels and then, on the Sunday, both Turkey v Italy in Arnhem and Holland v the Czechs at the Amsterdam Arena. They're both members of the Official England Travel Club, but were nonetheless unsuccessful in getting tickets for any of England's opening three matches because they hadn't yet accumulated enough points to entitle them to one. They had been granted vouchers for the quarter-finals and a place at the final should England qualify, but this just illustrates to me what a total waste of money it is joining the Official Club – unless, of course, you joined right at the beginning.

The problem is that 4800 tickets for 30,000 members just won't work, so you now have a catch-22 situation due to the creation of a new problem. I don't think anyone could argue against the points system brought in to ensure that the most loyal supporters get the first stab at the tickets. It's only fair that those who have followed England to every game, home and away, rather than just turning out for the big tournaments like I and many others do, should get looked after first and foremost. But with every game that passes, the difference in their points-total and the points-totals of all those not getting tickets lower down the ladder widens that little bit further, so eventually any new member will just be wasting their money because they'll have no real chance of ever catching up. If all you want to do is watch England at Wembley then yeah, fine, join the club – though when you consider the fact that getting tickets for Wembley games is easier than winning away at Chester this still seems like throwing good money after bad. Sally and Alan have in fact got all their Euro 2000 tickets through work connections – including two tickets for each of the England fixtures – which begs the question why they joined the Club in the first place.

As the train reaches the outskirts of the Dutch capital, a wonderful sight looms up on the horizon; Amsterdam Arena, the home of Ajax FC and the new national stadium. What a building! It's only upon seeing such an impressive sight close up that you realise how shite Wembley actually is. Alan tells me that the stadium is even more impressive inside and that the facilities as well as the atmosphere generated there are the best he has ever experienced. Let's hope that come 2 July we'll all be there together, roaring the England team on to a most glorious victory. Up until now the couple have done all their travelling by car, but Alan explains that the Dutch driving has put him off. He adds that someone on the motorway had come up his arse at 150 mph, which reminds Keef and I more of something we saw in the sex shop earlier this morning than of a near miss in a Volkswagen Polo.

Over an hour later the train hits the outskirts of Eindhoven, and for the first time the adrenalin starts to pump. This is what the trip's all about. Slowly the train passes by the PSV stadium – another impressive arena and the venue for the match. As we peer out of the window all we can see is the red, white and blue of England in the streets leading up to the ground. Eventually the train grinds to a halt and we pour onto the platform.

'ING-GER-LAND, ING-GER-LAND, ING-GER-LAND.'

Oh, I fucking love this. It's just like the old days. The old days of being on the football specials going to Crewe, Bolton and

Carlisle. The arms are out wide, pride pounds away in my chest and I've got a smile wider than a baboon's ring-piece. Keef is busy taking it all in while the locals look on, a mixture of shocked horror and smiling admiration etched across their faces. Following football is just the business when it's like this. It's a buzz like nothing else. No drug, no sexual exploit, no *nothing* can give you this particular high. This sense of belonging, camaraderie, pride and passion. It's wonderful, truly wonderful. If you have never experienced this feeling then I urge you to make the effort. Forget all the pre-tournament don't-travel-without-a-ticket bullshit. Forget the warnings spouted by MPs who are just desperate for media exposure, just get up and make the effort. Believe me, you won't be disappointed.

As we leave the station two local guys are offering tickets to anyone prepared to listen, but not even the police seem bothered by their efforts as they welcome us on to the streets of their town. The roundabout outside the station is littered with England flags. The atmosphere hanging over the town is relaxed, and most of the lads already well and truly pissed. Like the fans, the police seem at ease as they mingle with the crowds, their stance relaxed rather than aggressive – much the same as it was in Amsterdam the previous night. On various street-corners some of the local entrepreneurs are busy trying to palm off their cheap pre-match merchandise, but all most people want is beer. Not wishing to swim against the tide, Keef and I decide to join them and head off in search of a bar where we can get a few pints and hopefully watch the Germans get mullered by the Romanians at the same time.

My radar is off target once again and our search unfortunately leads us away from the main square and into a bar opposite a small church. (I say unfortunately because I later found out that two Dutch porn stars known as Tona and Kate were in the square giving it the large one, whereas the most exciting thing we saw was some fat bloke drooling behind nine pints of lager.) We bump into the lads from Birmingham again and I really want to ask the Albion fan among them whether or not he's aware that the Baggies' supporters have just been voted the scruffiest fans in Britain according to a poll I saw in the *Match of the Day* magazine. But considering he is currently wearing better clothes than I've ever possessed and looks quite hard, I think better of it. Outside the bar there are lads from Bournemouth, Villa, Stoke and Norwich, to name but a few, but on seeing a rather large Cross of St George with 'Dunstable' emblazoned across the front I think I'll move inside and finally watch some football. Keef soon gets talking to a lad from Doncaster who supports both Donny Rovers and Leeds. He tells us that one Sunday newspaper back home printed a map of Eindhoven indicating the locations of every Turkish bar, something which if true is nothing less than filth aimed at kicking things off so the media can get the story they so desperately want.

Somehow the Germans manage to get a 1–1 draw, even though they look shit while the Romanians don't look half bad. The final whistle also indicates that the time has come to leave the bar and head off up towards the ground. Now, when I am back home I very rarely drink beer because quite frankly I am a poor drinker, a four-pint Wendy, a shandy-drinking, southern softy. And I've never really been one for drinking at football, either, because I'd rather stay on the ball than be a soft target for some plod on a mission. I've seen so many lads get nicked at football for little else than being shit faced. They suddenly find themselves charged with being the leader of the pack and once the magistrate's been told they were drunk, that's it. However, the second I cross the water I go mad, thinking of myself as the world's number-one, top-banana drinking-machine, so by the time we turn to leave the bar I'm well and truly slaughtered. So much for the low-strength alcohol!

Thankfully everyone is heading in the same direction, like rats following some invisible Pied Piper, and there's a real buzz of anticipation filling the air. I check my ticket once again, only this time I notice that where the name of the original ticket-owner should be printed the word 'Portugal' stares back instead! *Portugal*? Keef, we're in the Portugal part of the ground ...

Suddenly we've got a potential problem. In the build-up to the tournament, the police and UEFA had made a big play in their statement that unless you can prove that your ticket belongs to you, you will in be turned away at the turnstile. They tried this tactic in France but it proved to be bullshit. However, if they do ask me to prove my Portuguese origin, things might just become a little difficult! Then I remember that Keef's girlfriend Moggie is Spanish – OK, I know it's a different language, but in my current state this seems the best option we have. At the very least it might have us sounding a little bit Diego-ish! Unfortunately, despite four years of living together, Keef can offer only a poor Manuel-of-*Fawlty Towers* '*Que*', so we resort to plan B and begin to act Dutch. 'We's expectings shome sexshe English footballs from yous guysh tonights, yesh?' Our impression is obviously more convincing than we expected. Maybe it's the beer making us slur even more, but when some poor sod asks if we are pleased that the England fans have behaved well while in *our* town, Keef can't help but reply: 'How the fuck do I know what's happening in Enfield right now?'

Suddenly we come to a halt as we reach the first barrier. Everyone – and I mean *everyone* – is English, but this isn't the official England end. Slowly the crowd filters through; a lad looks at our tickets and points us off towards the green section. No questions, just: 'Hello, yous enjoys the game.' We race towards the concrete steps that lead us up to our seats, and for the first time set our eyes on the lush green turf. What a sight. The four stands flanking the pitch look awesome. Why can't we build stadiums like this in England? Sunderland's Stadium of Light, the Reebok Stadium at Bolton and Derby's Pride Park lack so much compared to this. The atmosphere is electric. We look down to our left where the Portuguese supporters are doing their best to make themselves heard, bouncing up and down waving their scarves and singing their hearts out. In truth they stand no chance. The rest of the Philips Stadium rocks to the tune of the red, white and blue. England here, England there, England every fucking-where. And this is meant to be a Portuguese section! The St George Cross hangs from every possible vantage point. Behind us flies the flag of 'ull City FC and every team in England is represented in some form or another. The George Cross, England's flag, I love it. The Scots, the Irish and the Welsh will be doing nothing but sitting at home and having to take it all in. The thought of knowing they'll be desperate for us to lose somehow makes all this even better. You see, it's all they have left: envy. England are here, having it, taking part, while they just sit at home dreaming.

As ever, England's 5000 official tickets have turned into 20,000 fans No other country can do this. No other national football team can generate this level of support when they leave their own shores. Suddenly the teams enter the arena and the noise-level becomes almost deafening. I look at the players, the hopes of a nation resting on their shoulders as they jostle and bounce their way forward then line up and pay respect for the national anthems. What a responsibility! What a chance to shine! What lucky, lucky bastards those lads are! 'God Save the Queen' resonates around the metal and concrete arena, sending a shiver down my spine and a rush of blood through my veins. I stand proud, silent, as I take it all in. The players then break away, finish their stretches and line up in formation. The whistle blows, the crowd bellow one last encouragement and the waiting is over. England start well. The passing is crisp, the movement sharp. But the Portuguese look good themselves; their players aren't worried by the vast English support. Every English tackle is greeted by appreciative cheers, cheers that give way to yet another chorus; 'ING-GER-LAND, ING-GER-LAND, ING-GER-LAND . . .'

Below us, David Beckham receives the ball. Those who chose to sit now rise as one to join the rest of us, the guy sitting next to me grabbing my arm to help himself up. The England number 7 moves forward, drops his shoulder, and creates space. He draws back his right leg and sends the ball curling towards the goal-mouth. A flash of white darts forward; the keeper remains rooted to his goal; the curling ball dips and then . . . bang. In a flash the ball crashes against the underside of the crossbar then ricochets down behind the thick white line. For an instant I think to myself that no one else saw it. It was a goal, no one else realises it bounced behind the fucking line! Then the ball shoots up, sending a ripple across the roof of the net. My body explodes; 'GOOOOAAAALLLL! YESSSS! YOU BEAUTY!'

Three sides of the stadium erupt as the England players peel away to celebrate their prize. The arena goes mental, everyone around me embraces. Blokes who've never met before jump on each other's backs like a bunch of rabid hyenas on heat. The mixture of noise and emotion is unbelievable. England have scored, it's 1–0 to the England and just three minutes have passed. When the slightest ripple of calm descends I ask the bloke next to me who scored the goal. When he tells me it's Scholes I swear never again to abuse a gingger – unless of course he's Scottish. Suddenly my mind returns to sensible mode and begins to think the inevitable thought: 'OK, 1–0 – that'll do. Now blow the whistle, ref!'

The minutes tick by. The England fans are in full cry, but the Portuguese players slowly regain their composure and once again begin building their attacks from the back, their patient, passing football slowly easing their tension. Whenever England gain possession the mood rapidly changes and the pace quickens. With each pass, with each challenge, the English fans roar their approval, almost willing the ball forward. Down below, the ball once again arrives at Beckham's feet. In a flash the ball finds itself whipped into the penalty box, a carbon copy of what's gone before. Perfect. It curls between the defenders and the keeper. An outstretched leg connects and then, like my body, the white net bursts.

'YESSSSS!'

I suddenly find myself three rows down. I am jumping over seats in order to find someone, anyone, with whom to share this moment. I am bellowing at the top of my voice, although what I am saying is anybody's guess because I am lost in a mixture of frenzied ecstasy and pure abandonment. Nothing else on the planet exists at moments like this. Everything I've ever known, experienced, hated or loved is, for a few golden moments, forgotten. I am here, it's now, and it's two-fucking-nil!

Down to my right there lives a different world. A world almost burned out. There is no emotion from the Portuguese supporters, no movement, just silence. I can't help but taunt them, laugh at them. I know how they feel. Lord knows I've been there, every football supporter has been *there*. I think of the lads back home, how must they be feeling? Our green and pleasant land must be bouncing to the sound of one big party. Eventually I clamber back to my seat and find Keef wearing that wide-eyed grin once again. We share the moment, congratulate each other and join in the singing. Slowly my mood changes. I stare down on to the pitch as pride flows through my veins, pride accompanied by the thoughts that begin flowing through my mind: *'We're fantastic, we really are. We're going to win 4 or 5–1 and then go on to win the trophy. I know it. This is the moment it all begins. England's time has come, and I'm here to witness its birth!'*

I am convinced. They look like they can play a bit, but we're 2–0 up. We're going to be Euro 2000 champions! I feel a glow wash over me, a glow of contempt for all that lies before us. Oh, this is going to be fun! England's moment has arrived.

Figo, the Portuguese number 7, collects the ball and moves forward: *'Figo, heard so much about him, so what!'* In what looks like desperation he lines up a shot. *'He's trying to beat David Seaman from thirty yards. What a wan . . .'* For a split-second, time stands still. Then the bulging net gives the game away: *'He scored! Lucky bastard.'* I turn to Keef but offer no words, no emotion, just the raising of an eyebrow and a shrug of the shoulder. He says nothing. I convince myself of the insignificance of the moment, this goal being nothing more than a mere blip on our trail to glory. *'Let 'em have it. We'll score again anyway.'* As I try to remain calm more songs are sung. Struggling to remain confident, I find myself checking the clock at more regular intervals then, following yet another stray pass, I find words spitting violently from my lips: 'FOR FUCK'S SAKE, ENGLAND, COME ON. THIS IS SHIT.'

In that moment my faith has vanished. Now it's the Portuguese who pass the ball better. It's they who move quicker, sharper and with more purpose. From the far side the ball flies towards the goal. There's a diving header, Seaman is beaten, ball and post connect and the net ripples once more: 2–2. Keef drops to his seat while I stand motionless, staring at the raided goal-mouth. From my right a volcano of noise erupts as the Portuguese fans hit bursting-point. All else is drowned out but I can't look. I don't want to look. My hand rubs across my face and I blow a deep breath; 'Why does this always fucking happen?'

The half-time whistle brings much-needed relief. Keef and I convince ourselves that during the break Keegan will get things sorted and that normal service will quickly be resumed. We are also forced to agree that the Portuguese are one hell of a team. We make our way downstairs and begin milling around the crowd. Segregation between the two sets of fans is non-existent: we all brush shoulders and exchange relieved gestures. As we wander about, Keef and I suddenly realise we're standing smack-bang behind the goal and right in the middle of the Portuguese supporters! No questions have been asked, no tickets checked and, alarmingly, no police are around to keep order should the worst happen. Milling around are more English lads – some lost, some having a look and sussing things out – and I can't help but think that the security will need to be a little tighter than this when England face Germany in five days time!

We return to our seats and the second half begins. As each minute passes the inevitable seems to draw closer. England are getting overrun, outplayed and outclassed. My thoughts have changed. 'A draw will do. This is a good side, so a draw will do.' The Portuguese move even faster now, so quick. The ball cuts across the pitch to the far side, splitting the defence. 'No! Get there, Adams, get there.' Their forward latches on to the ball; his first touch is superb. Such pace, such skill. Then a flick with the outside of the right foot and . . . Goal! And what a goal – sheer class. The Portuguese fans go crazy, racing forward to climb the fence in celebration. Behind them the bank of supporters dance and hug each other as we had done before, their world now a wonderful place compared to the pit in which I find myself. This time I watch their celebration, and in a perverse way I force it upon myself. I can take it. I am used to it . . . I am fucking *English*, after all.

Now the clock runs more quickly, but rather than denying England anything, this rush of time saves us from the possibility of falling even further behind. From the stands, the supporters give everything but the team has nothing with which to repay our faith. The Portuguese toy with our team, take the piss. Eventually the final whistle blows, putting an end to our misery, an end to the humiliation, an end to the dream. As we turn to leave I can't but help take one last envious look at the Portuguese fans and wonder what it must be like to have a team such as that to follow. In the streets leading towards the train station, the England supporters talk in almost stunned admiration. At the station we bump into Don and my friend Melvin. We run the game over and over but the conclusion is always the same: we were simply beaten by a much better team. The train back to Amsterdam is crammed, and we find ourselves squashed together like a tin of unhappy sardines. Keef finds space by climbing up on to the parcel-shelf from where he declares himself innocent of Don's charge that he was the school bully. Meanwhile the lads below roll a spliff and pass it around to those who want it. There is no aggression, no anger. Just a desire to reach our respective destinations and forget what has happened.

From the Central Station we drift once more towards the red light district, where we are soon tempted into a small bar by some ropy black hooker. Tonight there is no hotel for Keef and me, because with a 5.30 a.m. train to catch we felt it best we save our money for more important things – such as beer and more beer. So while one of the lads seems flattered by the attentions of some saggy old whore, the rest of us set about the task of drowning our sorrows. By now I've had enough. All I want is to get back home, climb into bed and sleep off the last forty or so hours. We constantly pose the same question to each other: 'Why do England always do this?' but not one of us has the answer. At 2.30 the barman kicks us out. It's cold now; we're drunk and the red lights have lost their sparkle. Keef and I stop for a piss, but before I can feel the pleasure I spot three Dutchski policemen swaggering slowly towards us. Luckily I manage to hold it in, but for Keef the straining of the greens has already started. I scoot off laughing to rejoin the others and leave him at their mercy. As I shift away I can hear him begging for forgiveness. Five minutes later he turns the corner to give me the bollocking I deserve. It transpires that the coppers were on the look-out for an easy knock. First they had requested his passport and then asked whether or not he had any money. They had then asked if *I* had any money and when Keef pointed out that I had run off and left him they just laughed before saying, 'Well, it'sh a night ins the schlammers for yoush then, mister!'

Following which Keef had then pleaded stupidity and was eventually told in no uncertain terms to F-off!

As the hours pass, we find ourselves sharing the streets with no one but the druggies and drop-outs, so split from the others and head back to the station where we join a handful of English lads, a few travellers and the odd prostitute looking for a last bending. At last our train departs and it's time for kip. At 7.15 a.m. I am violently shaken by some Dutch guy on his way to work. I sit bolt upright to discover we have arrived at the Hook of Holland port and that the other England lads have gone off without waking either of us from our slumber. Four and a half hours later we're on a train heading out of Harwich and back towards Londinium. As we stare from the window at the rolling hills of England, Keef suddenly offers up some thought-provoking observations: 'Holland's countryside's dull as fuck, ain't it?'

There follows a moment's pause, then; 'Oh well, I know we lost but at least there weren't no trouble!'

Well fuck me! He was right an' all!

PART THREE
Germany

14

The Pains in Spain

Tuesday 13 June 2000

After a few hours' much-needed kip, I wake to learn that the great English press have slaughtered the team and butchered Keegan. These people sicken me. There is no honour, no willingness to accept defeat with grace, and no bowing to the fact that it was actually one hell of a game. All they can do is throw up their hands in disgust, point the finger and spit out their venomous headlines. The media smell blood. Even Gary 'I-don't-even-fart-in-the-bath, me' Lineker goes all Paxman on the England boss, questioning his tactics live on television and rocking him still further. Keegan looks like a man under immense pressure, and yet in one sentence he sums up the match perfectly: 'We were beaten by a better team in the second half.'

Well, you can't say fairer than that. At least he's honest. Unlike those who have gone before him, I don't feel like Keegan's treating me like some idiot, a no-brain who was watching a different game to the one that he witnessed. Don't get me wrong, I am well fucked off with the result, but Keegan knows he messed up – the difference being that he's big enough to hold up his hands and admit it, and for that I feel I must respect the man's honesty. And if it's time to come clean then I'll join the club myself: too right, throwing away a 2–0 lead at that level of the game is almost unforgivable but unfortunately it happens. It's another example of the beauty and the pain of following football. It's such unpredictability that has us turning up in our thousands week after week. Maybe I am getting old, going soft, turning all Dale Winton, I don't know, but I'll console myself with the fact that for twenty minutes we weren't that bad. I've come to terms with the fact that we ain't the best team in the world. Thirty-four years jack shit is enough to tell anyone that. (Come to think of it, having to beat the Sweaties in the play-offs was a fair pointer as well.) But on the plus-side, at least we're here. We've got a chance to put it right and one thing's for sure: we weren't as bad as the Germans were when they played Romania.

Keegan isn't the only one on the back foot: David Beckham once again seems to be taking up more than his fair share of the column-inches because he gave a section of England fans the old one-fingered salute!

However, if I thought the English press were enjoying Kev's downfall, then a quick look at the Spanish papers suggests that they have not only shot their bolt following Englands defeat, but are already reaching for the next handful of Kleenex, with Seaman – David Seaman, that is – being the main target for their abuse. Obviously still smarting from our penalty shoot-out victory over them during Euro '96, they now seek their revenge by blaming England's defeat fairly and squarely on the England number-one and our hero of the hour four years back: 'England would have done better if they had played with a goalkeeper' bleated the headline from one sports paper, while another referred to Seaman as 'A piece of meat with eyes'.

Ah the Spanish, a well-balanced race with a great sense of humour. However, the man upstairs moves in mysterious ways: later on in the day Spain lose 1–0 to the mighty Norway. In my mind I conjure up a vision of David Seaman pruning his moowie and offering a wry smile as the Vikings' goal follows an out-rageous blunder by – you guessed it – the Spanish goalkeeper,

Francisco Molina. Oh, and Spain play dreadfully – even Des Lynam takes the piss!

The other match taking place today is the one no one wants to see, Yugoslavia v Slovenia. In most people's eyes these two are only here to make up the numbers, and true to form they go out and produce the game of the tournament so far. The football flows from end to end in a match littered with great skill and outrageous mistakes before the Slovenians race into a 3–0 lead. Prior to kick-off the Yugoslavian coach, Vujadin Boskov, had stated that if Slovenia were to beat his side 'it wouldn't be a surprise; it would be a national catastrophe', and with less than twenty-five minutes to go, and following the sending-off of star player Mihajlovic, he could be seen flicking through the property pull-out of the local rag and ringing up the missus telling her to get on the first plane out of Belgrade. This is before his side in an amazing finale score three goals in less than six minutes! Not only does this level the score, it also saves Boskov's arse and no doubt pulls the plug on some Flemish estate-agent's Christmas bonus all in one go! Wonderful.

The highlight of the day comes when the Dutch authorities announce that they have nothing but praise for the England fans present in both Eindhoven and Amsterdam, and state that we would be welcomed back with open arms. One leading police officer is at pains to point out that the smoking of a nice spliff often curbs violent tendencies, somewhat backing up the plan offered up earlier by my good friend Dave. However, as the English news reporters begrudgingly join in the praise, they can't resist ending every item with the question they think everyone wants to hear: 'Will the good behaviour continue when England go head to head with Germany at the weekend?' Well, I wonder!

15

Lads, Leave the Becks Alone – It'll Go to Your Head

Wednesday 14 June 2000

The big news today involves David Beckham and his one-finger gesture to the England fans as he left the pitch in Eindhoven. The papers that were so quick to jump on his back are now turning to his defence following the disclosure of what the taunts were that forced such a reaction – and you'll not find me having a pop at the press in this particular instance. I'll admit that had I seen the gesture and been reporting for one of our daily nationals, I too would have slaughtered our number 7 and condemned his actions as a disgrace. But the headline staring back at me today truly beggars belief: 'YOUR WIFE IS A WHORE AND WE HOPE YOUR KID DIES OF CANCER.'

Christ, that's nasty, vile beyond belief. In twenty-six years of following football I've never heard anything that even comes near that. In the pictures of Beckham accompanying the piece you can see a mixture of disbelieving hurt, anger and disgust etched into his features. Surely no man deserves that sort of taunting. The first part is bad enough, but *'we hope your kid dies of cancer'* – what kind of idiot has the brain even to *think* something like that? Usually the only argument I have with supporters who abuse players is one based on getting them to shut up so that I can have a good go myself. To me it's part of football. If a player's shit then I'll be the first to tell him. I believe I am entitled to tell him. I've paid my money and I therefore expect a performance.

There'll be many people disgusted at such comments: they hate the verbal and detest the abuse. Well, if I perform like a twat at work, someone soon sends a rocket up my arse (and if truth be told, I should be orbiting Mars by now) but I have to get on with it. Sorry, folks, but the verbal comes with the territory as far as I am concerned. The second you pop your head over the side of the trench people line up to shoot you down. Believe me, I know. I get enough flack myself just for *writing* about the game. During the last four years I've been branded just about everything. The far left have had a dig at me and so have the far right, when in reality I don't give a fuck about politics. I've been accused of hating women – again bullshit; I think every bloke should have one. My work has even been labelled homophobic, for Christ's sake! OK, so I prefer Homer Simpson videos to homosexual ones, but I ain't going to apologise for being straight. Anyway, I've got a gay mate and we get on fine. He comes and cleans the flat while I change his spark plugs! Everyone's happy.

I've slagged Beckham in the past and daresay I'll do it again. I'd slag any player who I felt posed a threat to my team, and I'd do it in the hope that it would put him off his game. But to bring such sickening comments regarding the man's children into the arena is overstepping the mark by a million miles. The thing I struggle to understand about this incident is that on the night Beckham was by far and away our best player. He chased everything, made both goals and stood head and shoulders above anyone else wearing the white shirt of England. Apparently some people feel Beckham is carrying an even greater weight; that of the domestic team he plays for back home. Ted Beckham, David's father, was sitting right among those 'fans' hurling the comments towards his son, and accuses those involved of simply hating anything connected to Manchester

United (both Philip and Gary Neville also came in for stick from those around him). I would certainly agree that there is an element of anti-United feeling within the England following, something clearly illustrated by the fact that a chorus of 'Stand up if you hate Man-U' could be heard ringing around the stadium on at least one occasion that night. Personally, I've always felt that the second you cross the water, all the home front grudges should be left behind as we all come together as England, but there are some – such as Danny from Burnley – who feel Manchester United and a few of their players get everything they deserve:

I hate them. I hate what they have done to English football. Their greed has ruined the game in this country and now all they want to do is leave the English behind. They virtually control the game here now. The media daren't have a go at them. The FA are scared shitless of them and the media seem to believe that the world stops once you set foot outside Old Trafford. Every paper is 'United this, United that'. They have them over a barrel because if the press fuck them off, United just close the door and shut up shop. They have worked themselves into a position where they hold the rest of us to ransom. What they did by pulling out of the FA Cup was a scandal. They should never have been allowed to get away with it. Even their own fans thought that was disgraceful. It was all so calculated – pure psychology over everyone else – and the FA played right into their hands. Chelsea didn't win the FA Cup, just some Year 2000 Mickey Mouse trophy that United couldn't be bothered to enter. It meant nothing last season. All that bollocks about pressure from the FA! Man-U are bigger than the FA, for Christ's sake. They could have told them to stick it but no, they let the FA believe they were flexing their muscles when really United were pulling the strings all along. They were so clever in making it look like they had no choice and the FA swallowed it. They've fucked that competition now. United could easily have fielded a team – look at the size of their squad. Their reserves would beat most sides outside the Premiership easy; it was all bullshit.

Pretty soon they will do the same to the league; they'll piss off and leave the rest of us to pick up the pieces because that is where the money is, and money is all that matters to them. That's why people hate Man United – because of their greed. They're fucking the rest of us over just to make a few more pounds. They want out and don't give a toss about the rest of us. But if you fuck people over then those people turn on you and that's why they get so much stick. When you hear United fans talk they will tell you that the most important thing now is winning the Champions League, not the Premiership; they don't care about it anymore. They are so arrogant; believing that winning the Premiership is just a matter of going through the motions. The saddest thing is they're not wrong and we all know it.

When you look at the crowd at Old Trafford now, there are rows of Japanese and Scandinavians rather than Englishmen – what good is that for English football? And how can the rest of us ever hope to hang on to a side who can even *consider* spending nineteen million pounds on just one player? The gap is getting bigger every year and soon we will have the same situation as they have in Scotland. Virtually every year it's a one-horse race. Once a team gets that far ahead there is no chance of catching them. Our only pleasure comes on the one or two times a season they fuck up and get beat! But even when that happens they can't accept it. The way they react! Is it any wonder that people despise them? They get away with murder and the FA do nothing. They just run scared. They know United could pull the plug at any time and so they get away with chasing referees, abusing the crowd and kicking the shit out of the opposition. It's one set of rules for United and another for the rest of us. It sickens me, it really does.

United are the biggest team in the world. Worldwide,

there're bigger than Juventus, Barcelona and Real Madrid put together. They have supporters' groups in every part of the globe. Every week at Old Trafford there are thousands of Irish and Jocks who obviously couldn't give a toss about England or the England team, and those fans obviously have some influence on the club. Do they want England to win? Do they bollocks. That is where all this anti-United stuff comes from, as those fans believe that United are more important than the England team. Those fans don't want the likes of Scholes and Beckham fucking off on international duty, and once they start moaning others join in. Eventually it seeps right through the club, right to the top – and let's face it, England winning doesn't put the pounds on United's share-value, does it!

Worldwide, United may well have more support than England, but not on these shores, no fucking way, and that's why there's this hate. They may like to think they are, but Man-U aren't bigger than the England team; no one is. I am Burnley through and through, but the truth is that you can choose your football team but you are born into your country. Your nationality is given to you and nothing is more important than your place of birth. It's the one thing we all share, being English. Manchester United have become such a monster that their biggest problem seems to be that Manchester happens to be in England and their side play in the English league. But if the United fans and players think they're getting stick now, then they're in for a nasty surprise once they fuck off to join the European league. You wait to see what happens then!

Some would argue that the abuse concerning David Beckham, his wife and their marriage is in many ways self-inflicted, an undesired spin-off fuelled by the couple's constant media manipulation. However, involving their child in that abuse surely reaches depths that not even the most broad-minded among us find acceptable. Keegan, too, came to the defence of his star player, claiming to be outraged by what he had heard and praising Beckham for keeping calm when others might well have cracked. The England manager also asked what were these people hoping to achieve at a time when England needed their star player? It's a question that no one but those involved can answer. All I can say is that it was a good job he played well. As for the abuse directed at the Neville brothers, well, come on, Kev – they probably deserved it.

Back at the competition, the hosts Belgium are taking on Italy. For the Italian nation this match provides a poignant moment because it means a return to the redeveloped King Baudouin Stadium, the arena previously known as Heysel. There, prior to the 1985 European Cup final between Liverpool and Juventus, thirty-nine people lost their lives following violent clashes between the two sets of supporters. The disaster led to a ban on English clubs taking part in European football and should have been a catalyst towards ridding the game of football hooliganism once and for all. And yet amazingly we find ourselves some fifteen years on in a situation where the Belgian authorities are setting up temporary morgues because a football match is taking place! Italy win the game 2–0 but the final whistle brings with it more violence. As supporters from both sides make their way towards the Bourse in the city centre, they begin to clash. One unfortunate fan is hit with a firecracker; bottles and chairs are sent flying through the air and attacks are made on passing vehicles. Drivers and passengers are soon trapped in their cars while hooligans jump on their roofs and smash shop windows. After a long delay the Belgian police finally spring into action as the rampaging threatens to escalate out of control. A total of twenty-five people are arrested before order is finally restored. But for the police officers of Brussels, this incident will prove to be nothing more than a brief warm-up for the events about to come their way . . .

16

Anything Good on TV, Love?

Thursday 15 June 2000

For the English football fan, the main talk today is not of the tournament but rather the new television deal struck by football's leading ladies and gentlemen, a deal that sounds the death-knell for that great British institution *Match of the Day*. As the BBC lose out, ITV take over in the fight for terrestrial domination after clinching a three-year deal worth a staggering £180 million. BSkyB's continued involvement – at an outrageous cost of £1.1 billion – ensures that Friday and Monday nights will for the time being remain a toil for those of us who prefer to watch their football live and in the flesh. As will our Sunday mornings, afternoons, early evenings or whenever it is that they want their games to be broadcast!

While the players and their agents head off for a cold shower and a rub down with *Sporting Life* to calm their delight, the fans can console themselves with the notion that such an injection of money might well stall the inevitable approach of the European Super League for at least a few more years. Added to that the fact that the pairing of both Alan Hansen and Mark Lawrenson will soon be banished from our screens, and suddenly life doesn't seem so bad after all!

Meanwhile, back at the tournament Turkey and Sweden

draw 0–0. Wow, if only all football on television could be like that . . .

17

Women, Just a Bunch of Old Pros

OK, folks, it's quiz time. In March 2000 the Football Association announced in their 'Blueprint for the Future' their intention to set up a professional Women's League by the year 2003, a declaration that both took me by surprise and had me checking my solar-chart in order to reassure myself I actually inhabit the same planet. And so it is with that in mind, and purely in the interest of research, that I set you the following multiple-choice questions. Right, eyes down and here we go:

Question 1:
How would you describe the playing-standard of women's football in this country?

(a) Shite.
(b) Not very good, really. Piss-poor at best.
(c) Highly skilful, very exciting and in no way useless. It's really catching on, you know.

Question 2:
How many people, on average, do you think actually attend a women's football match in England?

(a) Er, well, fuck all, really. A few kids 'cause the crèche is shut, some lezzers and a bloke who's probably not good enough to train a blokes' team. Oh, and the odd pervert, of course.

(b) About the same as you'd get watching a half-decent Sunday pub-side, but no more.

(c) Oh, lots and lots, honest. It's really catching on, you know.

Question 3:

What do you think of the Football Association's proposal for setting up a professional Women's League by the year 2003?

(a) Ha ha ha . . . Hang on, you're not fucking serious, are you?

(b) Well, it seems stupid to me but hey, this *is* the year 2000.

(c) A most excellent idea and about time too because it's really catching on, you know.

Question 4;

Do you think women's football will ever catch on in England?

(a) Will it bollocks! . . . Unless they do it nude, of course – then I'd go.

(b) Yes, probably, but only on the playing front. I can't see it turning into a big spectator-sport, not with men's football being as strong as it is.

(c) Oh God, yes. Pretty soon we will see women competing alongside men. They'll play in the same leagues, a woman will pick up the FA Cup and go on to captain the national side one day, I am sure, because it really *is* catching on, you know.

Now check your score:

If you have mostly answered (a) to the above questions, then you are probably a bit of a geezer. You think only blokes should play football and you enjoy pies, porn and Peter Beardsley, because you think you're better looking than he is.

If your answers have been mostly (b) then you are probably much the same as those who answer mostly (a) but like to think of yourself as having a bit of that 'new man' bollocks about you – i.e. you do the washing-up every Thursday. You also come across as being someone who likes to say two words when one will do and prefer to voice a well-thought-out opinion when surely the answers indicated by (a) would have been more than enough, thank you very much.

And finally, if you have mostly given the answers (c) then you're probably already working within the Football Association's 'let's pander to the minority' department along with all the other (c)s who think up such bullshit proposals.

Well, how did you do? For me it's (a) all the way across, and if by chance you happen to agree, can I request you cut out your answers and send them on a postcard to Lancaster Gate requesting they stop wasting money and start sorting out the problems that currently embarrass the nation – i.e., the men's England international team. And I say that not out of any hatred for women's football, but rather out of a sense of reality and the need to distribute the pot of money fairly instead of indulging in some pointless politically correct public-relations exercise.

Let me state here and now that I have absolutely nothing whatsoever against women playing football. OK, so I think it's crap and I wouldn't watch it as long as I've got a hole in my arse, but I am not exactly Pelé myself. It's just that at a time when some of our league clubs dice with their very existence, I find such a commitment from the FA both hard to understand

and more than a little insulting to the many male professionals currently living week to week wondering whether or not their club is actually about to go into liquidation. The need to develop the women's game is not something I bring into question because, like all grass-roots football in this country, it needs all the help it can get. However, just why the FA feel they need to make the women's game 'professional' in a day and age when making money rules beats me.

Football is as much about share-prices as it is anything else, and therefore such a commitment appears to make about as much business-sense as would buying out the patents and re-introducing the Sinclair C5 to our streets. Crowds smaller than a Wimbledon reserves match, no real interest from the vast majority of fans already watching men's football, and recent television figures indicating less interest than for an *Eldorado* re-run all suggest that the call for a professional Women's League in this country is ridiculous in the extreme. And then there's the fact that many of our established lower-league clubs continually toy with the idea of going part-time – you have to decide whether or not someone at Lancaster Gate is displaying the tactical genius of a baboon.

The FA base some of their commitment to the women's game on the fact that almost thirty per cent of the crowds now seen at football is female. This argument quite frankly holds about as much water as a camel with a javelin through its back and has absolutely no relevance whatsoever to the point in hand. Just because people *watch* a sport doesn't mean they wish to partake themselves. Personally, I love rugby league but I would never dream of playing the game (I'd get killed). And, of course, being a bloke I also like to watch a fair bit of women's tennis. I like watching women's tennis for many reasons, one of which I'll admit is more obvious than most and something that leaves me open to the same kind of jibes the girlies receive when gawping at male footballers' legs. Thing is, I don't mind owning up to it. Oh yes, I like to see a girl stretch all right. (Just the thought of that Russian sort has me breaking out into a sweat, and it's not the planting of an ace in the other girl's box I am thinking of when she smashes one over the net, oh no . . .) But the fact that I watch women's tennis doesn't make me want to go out and play a few sets myself; no way, José. However, if the Football Association do want to play the statistics game when they begin dishing out the funds, then might I suggest that the blokes' game at grass-roots level gets its own fair slice of the cake as well. Which, if my maths serve me right, adds up to . . . oh, seventy per cent, thank you very much!

Of course, champions of the women's game point to the success of leagues in such places as Italy and America, where players can earn good money and crowds turn out in the thousands – qualities that bode well for economic success. Admittedly, women's football is big in Europe, but as I've never trusted girls who don't shave their armpits I'll dismiss it for what it is: a sideshow to the main event. And as for America, well whoopee – so what? The main reason behind women's football's success in the USA is that, unlike in the rest of the world, the men's game has never really caught on there. Football is currently seen as a predominantly female sport in America and, owing to the popularity of the country's traditional sports, such as American football, basketball and baseball, it will always struggle to break free from that image. Indeed, some argue that the organisations behind the big three sports across the water openly encourage the women's game so as to avoid losing their traditional male support and players of the future. Over here the situation is very different. Football is *the* national game, ingrained at all levels of society, and so shall forever remain an overwhelmingly male-dominated sport. There is nothing on these shores that even comes close to football's popularity, and without such competition the public will demand the best. For which you can look only towards the male side of the sport.

Nevertheless, considering the current poor standard of play boasted by women's football, it hasn't actually done that badly for itself. Already clubs bend over backwards to accommodate the breasted devils. Players who wouldn't even make a shite Sunday-morning side already find themselves playing the game in some of the best stadiums the country has to offer, treading the holy turf and living out the dreams most football-loving blokes will never have the joy of experiencing. But as the clubs' PR departments clamber over themselves in search of eleven ladies and a child-minder, I can't help but feel that many are also opening up for themselves a can of worms the size of Stan Collymore's ego. The twentieth of April 2000 marked the introduction of the country's first professional women's football team as the Fulham chairman, Mohammed Fayed (God bless you, sir – just send the money in the post) staked his latest claim for world and football supremacy. But as he introduced his new £1000-a-week star player Margunn Haugenes (yes, you guessed it: Norwegian) to the press, it wasn't just the sound of applause that could be heard rippling down the Thames. There were also some uneasy mutterings emanating from every employer's worst nightmare, the Equal Opportunities Commission. Amazingly, the EOC immediately jumped on the bandwagon, reportedly stating that, 'If men and women do the same job in any other walk of life they have the right to the same pay and working conditions. And if they are playing and working to a comparable standard, for example in a fully professional league, then they would have the right to ask for the same earnings.' Obviously, were we to focus on the words 'comparable standard' within that statement, it could be argued that instead of warming up within the polished walls of Craven Cottage, most of the girls should be paying their three quid subs to cover their referee's fees and dropping their pre-match dumps down the same hell-hole of a toilet as the rest of us. But if we focus on the FA's favourite word, 'professional' . . . well, who knows where Mr Fayed could be heading.

With many clubs, including some of those at the very top of the game, presently cutting back on their reserve side, the vision of others scrambling to join such a shortsighted public-relations race seems like madness. If you're still in doubt as to just where the FA should be concentrating their efforts, I'll take the liberty of offering up yet another question in the hope of resolving the situation. OK, here goes:

Club X are shit. (For the purpose of the exercise let's call them L*t*n.) They can't score and are in desperate need of a new striker as their fans are restless and their shareholders more than a little pissed at the prospect of relegation. Unfortunately, the club's manager has no money to spend. Following the annual financial review, however, he discovers that the club has spent more money on funding the PR job that is its women's team than he needed to sign the aforementioned new striker. Which of the following words of advice do you think the club's fans and shareholders offer to the chairman on hearing the news?

(a) You dozy fucking twat. What the fuck do you think you're doing? Dump the tarts now and buy a new striker you daft cunt, or else we'll beat you so hard . . .
(b) As for (a)
(c) Oh well, never mind, But hey, cheer up – we got forty-seven fans in for the last women's game. It's really starting to catch on, you know.

So how did you do? Are you still a (c)? Oh well, never mind . . .

However, I do have something to offer those running the women's game in this country: over the last decade the women's game has come on by leaps and bounds – probably further than most could ever have expected – thus forcing the FA into sitting up and taking notice. As already stated, I believe the women's game in England has elevated itself to a status way above its standard of play and is currently enjoying a profile and facilities most men's sides would die for. For this I can only congratulate them. That said, I sincerely hope that those running the women's game are not daft enough to get sucked in by some PR stunt dreamed up by an organisation run predominantly by men, because it is a stunt that could well blow up in their faces and see the women's game taking as many steps back as it has already taken forward. If something within a football club has to give, you can bet your reinforced sports-bra that the fans won't let it be the men's first-team. With this in mind, those female teams clambering to affiliate themselves with league clubs would do well to remember just what happened to their male reserve- and youth-teams once the pursestrings tightened.

What is that piece of advice women always offer each other? Oh yeah: 'Remember, men will promise the world but all men are liars!' That's it. So, if the women's game in this country is to continue to prosper at its current rate, may I suggest the following to anyone presently steering it forward: take control of your own future, look after number one and never forget your own advice. After all, haven't women always been pretty good at keeping their own houses in order?

18

Stoking Up the Fire

Friday 16 June 2000

This proves to be one hell of a tough day. I had made the mistake of promising my wife that, having survived the beach battle at Marseille in '98, I would never again put myself in a situation where I might end up getting a good hiding, or something even worse. Thus, convincing her that England's match against Germany is going to be nothing but a tea party is proving to be a bit of a struggle. The early-morning news doesn't help my case. Reporters send back their piece from a campsite in Charleroi, where a small group of England fans tell a tale of local Turkish lads who are doing the rounds on bikes, sussing things out and giving it the big one. The item ends with some fresh-faced lad offering the sound bite: 'We'll fight back if attacked.' You can sense the reporter rubbing his hands together in anticipation. I can't help thinking I'll have to keep Mrs Brimson away from the television for the rest of the day.

Thankfully, I pack her off to work, which leaves me free to set about the task of sorting out my travel arrangements. Little does she know that a few weeks back I booked myself on to a EuroStar train departing Waterloo Station in the early hours of tomorrow morning, with the return-journey ticket booked for the morning after the Romania game. Now all I have to do is work out how to get back immediately after the fixture with Germany. Unfortunately, I'm having to travel to the game alone because all my mates are either scared of getting caught up in the trouble or simply felt that, with virtually no chance of getting a ticket, it's best to stay in Blighty and watch the game down the pub. I must admit that the possibility of serious trouble has made me think twice and that I find the prospect of travelling alone a bit daunting – especially when it's possible that trouble could kick off at any turn. During the last few weeks I've spoken to many lads who think I'm a real idiot for making the trip, my only answer being: 'But this is England versus Germany, I've got to go!' Anyway, watching the game back here could well turn out to be just as dangerous, particularly as the best option seems to be to watch it up at my local footy club Hemel Hempstead Town FC.

The offer of a big screen, a barbeque and a disco was well tempting, but for me it's been overshadowed by the fact that the entertainments manager has added a few exotic dancers on to the bill. (As if England v Germany wasn't enough of a pull on its own!) It's fair to say that up at HHTFC there are a few naughty lads, the kind of people you really wouldn't want to upset, and recalling the last time I attended a strip night at which some of these lads were also present has me thinking that a possible showdown with a few Germans is far less of a worry. The event in question was held at the local rugby league club where, having kept the lads waiting, the first stripper lasted no more than a minute before she got glassed off stage. (Apparently a few of the lads felt the poor girl's looks weren't up to scratch.) As for the rest of the cast, well, we didn't get to see any of them because they were already heading out the back door, half dressed and screaming at the top of their voices. And there was me worried about Fritz and his mates.

As ever, my dad is helping to settle my nerves by hitting the old panic-button, even going so far as to suggest that I grow a goatee beard so I won't get recognised and will look a little bit . . . softer! Recognised by whom? And since when has facial hair ever stopped a good right-hander? I'd rather have some Turk stab me in the back than look like some over-aged advertising executive, skateboarder hanging on to his youth. If anyone reading this is over thirty-five and has a goatee beard then please be offended – I am only saying what your friends are thinking. Try growing old gracefully, you sad bastard.

The press are also busy stoking the fire. One tabloid bleats out that more than 40,000 Englishmen and women are heading for the Low Countries, most without tickets, while another points to a press conference held by the Dutch Police Intelligence Service, or BVD as they are known. Their spokeswoman, Miranda Havinga, claims that English and Italian hooligans are joining up and plotting to stab Turkish fans in revenge for the killings in Istanbul! This claim clearly indicates that all police intelligence services throughout Europe speak the same international language: namely bullshit.

After making numerous phonecalls I eventually manage to secure a seat on an unofficial England supporters' coach that leaves for home directly after the match. Confirmation of this brings me untold relief – the thought of hanging around and sleeping rough on the streets of Belgium admittedly holds little comfort. At least now if things do go off big style, all I have to do is keep my head down, watch the clock and sit by the coach until home-time. All that's left to do today is relax and watch the footie.

Today's first match involves the French taking on the Czech Republic. During the match, commentator Barry Daves flies the flag like never before as he refuses to accept the fact that English referee Graham Poll and his lines man screwed up by giving the Czechs a very dubious penalty. Not even after watching the replay, which clearly showed the foul being committed well outside the penalty box, will big Baz admit the English official got it wrong. Not even when Trevor Brooking, of all people, questions his judgement will Bazzer relent, his only concession to say: 'Well, who would begrudge the Czechs their penalty?' Well, I imagine the French might have something to say about it while they sip their half-time cup of Bovril, Baz! But a nice bit of patriotism nonetheless.

Once again the Czech side end up losing a game they really should have won, and become the first team to get knocked out of the tournament. As for the French, the pundits all share the opinion that they are the best thing since being *fucked by fish*, whereas I personally would love to see them get knocked out as soon as possible. I say that because I have become tired of our domestic league's sudden fascination with all things garlic since their side became world champions. I don't deny their talent, but I get so fucked off with the constant whinging of the French players and managers who are currently earning a fair few squid on our shores. Indeed, even one of today's papers is carrying an article featuring a top French player – namely the Chelsea star Didier Deschamps – in which he and his family claim to hate living in England because it is always so cold. My reaction to this is: 'Well, go on then, Didier. Go on, fuck off and let some English lad have a run-out, you beret-wearing frog arse.' (Following Euro 2000 my request was upheld and Captain France departed the London club for Spain. How strange life is!)

Another bunch of unhappy Euros are the hookers of The Hague who have filed a complaint stating that the Euro 2000 finals are damaging their business. They are claiming that most of their regular punters are more concerned with getting home to watch the footy than with having a quick in-and-out stop on the way home from work. As this particular branch of the 'bury-me-in-a-Y-shaped-coffin girls' are only allowed to work during daytime hours, they have requested a special licence to enable them to put in a few hours overtime (or should that be under-time?). The local authority has unfortunately refused to grant them such a licence. The girls are not willing to take this decision lying down – well, not after 6.00 p.m., anyway!

Meanwhile, as night falls the Dutch enter the football arena for their second match of the championship, against the Danes. After an edgy start they cruise to a 3–0 victory, at times playing the kind of football once associated with their dream team of the 70s, while their supporters turn the De Kuip Stadium in

Rotterdam into one big orange bowl with a show of support any other nation would die for. When you see the Dutch national side being supported in such a manner, it makes it hard to believe that their domestic league has any kind of hooligan problem whatsoever, and yet with clubs such as Feyenoord, Ajax, Utrecht and Den Haag, they have some of the most active hooligan firms on mainland Europe. Feyenoord fans have a rivalry with Spurs that dates back to 1974, while in 1987 their fans went on the rampage when returning home from a UEFA Cup-tie with Aberdeen, wrecking a ferry along the way. Ajax of Amsterdam were banned from European competitions for two years following rioting by their fans during a cup-tie with FK Austria in the 1989–90 season; and four stabbings were reported during running battles between Juventus and Ajax supporters prior to the 1996 European Cup final. However, the most infamous incident involving Dutch fans came in 1997 when Ajax and Feyenoord supporters went head-to-head in a pre-arranged battle of sheer, unadulterated violence. The incident took place in a field outside the small town of Beverwijk, where it had been agreed that the top fifty lads from each firm would meet up in order to fight one another.

Those involved in setting up the 'off' had also agreed that neither side would come tooled-up for the fight, but unfortunately for the lads from Amsterdam it was only they who arrived willing to play by the rules. The Feyenoord firm outnumbered their rivals almost six to one and many of them came with weapons in hand. The Ajax lads stood no chance, and with little cover to head for they found themselves on the receiving end of a serious hiding – a hiding that saw one of their number beaten to death under a barrage of baseball bats and hammer–blows. The incident shook not only Dutch football but also the nation as a whole, and resulted in the jailing of eight people, all of whom were supporters of Feyenoord. This horrific event marks a black day in the rivalry between the two clubs, and the Dutch can only hope that on this occasion history does not repeat itself.

Back at home the telephone rings and a friend delivers the news I've been dreading: 'Have you heard? It's all kicked off in Belgium.' Well, that's me in for a good night's sleep, then – cheers, Dave! Unfortunately, he wasn't wrong. While I'd been sitting comfortably watching the Dutch game on television, Pete from West London had been watching his back in Brussels;

Everyone had been waiting for this; this was the big one and you just had to be there, you know what I mean? The media had been building it up and the police were getting silly. Mistake was, they were all talking about England versus Germany. This wasn't about Germany, this was about the Turks. Fuck the Germans – they were never going to show anyway, were they? Never have done. Come to think of it, I never saw one German all the time I was in Brussels!

Thing is it's not just the Turks, is it? It's the immigrants as well. Same as it was in Marseille. They'll have a go because they've got fuck to lose, have they? They had already played up with the local Old Bill and what with the Leeds/Arsenal thing it was always going to happen. But I never thought the Belgian police would turn out like that. They were bastards, the worst I have ever come across abroad by a mile. I'll admit I like a bit of a row, but once I saw what their coppers were like, that was it – I wanted out.

There was no chance of having a proper row with the Turks in the end anyway. We'd gone out on the EuroStar and got to Brussels around midday. We dropped the gear at the hotel then headed into the centre to find a decent bar, get beered up and have something to eat, then we joined up with a few other lads who'd been out since Eindhoven. Everywhere you went there were England lads; it was like we had taken the place over and you could tell, even that early, that the police weren't in the mood to mess around. They only seemed bothered by us, though – they didn't give a fuck about all the Turks and them going around and mouthing off. They didn't like it that England had turned up big-style – more than they expected, I reckon – and so they were well up for it. Giving it the big one, putting on a show. They were desperate to have it away with anyone in an England shirt.

It amazes me. It never changes when you travel with England. Everybody hates us, they always do. That's why a lot of lads get pissed off and end up having a go back. Every bar we went in, lads were saying it was going to kick off sooner or later as the local wankers had been mouthing off all day and a few things had kicked off the night before – nothing serious, just a few slaps and that. You'd think the Belgians would want a dig at them themselves, but they didn't give a shit; all they wanted was to have it away with England. The thing with the Turks is that you know they won't fight – they'd sooner stab you and be on their toes. You could end up getting knifed for just taking a wrong turn, so it's best to stay together and hang around where all the other lads are. During the day we had moved around a few bars, but the police then started trying to keep tabs on everyone and were trying to stop people leaving one bar for another. When that starts happening you know it's time to get out if you can, because all they are doing is trying to keep you penned in.

We'd actually got to that O'Reilly's at about half-six and you could see there was a fuck load of lads in there. Outside, the police were already mobbed up and waiting for them to kick off. It gets on your tits; I mean you can see why we get pissed off. The police line up in front of you, just waiting for it to happen, but let locals get on with it. Sometimes all you have to do is start singing back and they'll pull out the old truncheons and start giving it some. Everyone goes on about how we should behave, and that the English should have more respect whenever we go to another country. We *do* have respect; what's wrong with singing, for fuck's sake? It's what the English do. We sing because we're proud of our country, our history. The

English have more respect than any other country in the world, that's why everyone comes here. And it's why we rescued every other bastard during the war. We should have left them to speak fucking German. How much respect would they have then? Look at the Italians or the Norwegians; they're as loud as fuck but no one gives a shit! But we sing and the Old Bill think it's World War Three kicking off!

If they'd have just left us to it and kept the Turks away then I tell you, nothing would have happened at that bar. But the Belgian coppers loved it. Every one of them wanted to have it away with England, you could tell. The longer it went on, the more people got pissed off with having them in their faces, and at about seven o'clock you could tell the atmosphere turned right naughty 'cause they suddenly doubled the numbers and showed up big time. Suddenly there's vanloads of the bastards, all geared up and ready for a pop. We hadn't been there that long but when I saw that I thought best get out as it was going to go off any minute. So we moved out of the bar and got across the street. They knew most of the English were pissed up and so it's easy pickings, innit?

We were lucky, really, getting out when we did. Although it was well dodgy where we'd moved to because there were loads of Turks and Arabs around looking for it. Well naughty it was. All the camera crews were there as usual, the bastards. They know what goes on but they never tell the truth, do they? That's why everyone hates them. They didn't give a fuck about what the police or the Turks got up to. No, they're all focused on the bar because they know that's where all the good pictures are going to come from. Fuck what might be going on elsewhere with the Turks and the police winding all the England lads up. They don't give a shit.

I tell you, you needed eyes in the back of your head where we were. You had to watch the Turks, the Old Bill, keep an eye on who's coming and going. Fucking scary!

There's no point in doing the off. You turn up the wrong street and you could be taking a right hiding. No, you're best off staying put and keeping an eye on what's going on around you.

Rumour had been going around that they'd had loads of plain-clothes coppers out and about, picking people off and pointing out faces. If you get nicked you've had it, ain't you? It gets to being that every time you leave a bar and someone follows you out, you wonder who they are! You end up being wary of everyone. I don't want to be in a situation like that again in a hurry. It's exciting but it ain't half dodgy – when it kicked off, fuck me did it go off.

With the police not doing nothing about the Turks, the more of them that showed the more mouthy they got. It got to be a real piss-take. It wouldn't have surprised me if the police put them up to it. Sure as shit they used them as an excuse to start the ball rolling. They knew sooner or later someone would bite, and then when this small mob of Turks arrived all giving it large, that was it. They were giving it the right big 'un at the English lads in the bar. I don't blame anyone for having a go at those wankers; they deserved everything they got. They're carrying bits of metal and stuff and the police don't do anything at all, just let them get on with it. If the Old Bill would have clubbed a few of them instead, the English would have given them a round of applause. Everything would have probably been all right then, but they just left them to it! We were outside, right in among it, and for a while I was shitting myself. If they had turned on us out there, fuck knows what would have happened. A lot of people wanted away as soon as they saw they were carrying stuff, because everyone knows they carry knives and shit.

Then one Turkish geezer really went for it, all on his own, right up to the front of the bar, really going mental. He had some balls, I'll give him that. But that was it. That bar emptied in about half a second flat. Glasses and tables went flying. And the noise! Fucking hell! But as ever, when the English lads came steaming out the Turks fucked right off. Then that's it, the Old Bill have got what they wanted, ain't they, and they go mental. They piled right in. Not just in on the lads in the bar, either – everywhere. It was mad. Looking back on it, I don't know how they got away with it. I've never seen anything like that before; they were bang out of order. They didn't care who they hit, whether you wanted out or in, they just hit anyone they could get their hands on. If you were in the way you'd had it. I saw about ten seconds of it and that was enough; all I wanted was out.

People were running everywhere with coppers chasing them. Only me and one of the other lads managed to stay together; all the others got split from us. They legged it like most people, the coppers steaming down the road after them. There were all sorts of people – women, kids, old blokes – the coppers didn't give a fuck. People were running into the bars trying to get out of the way, but the police steamed in after them, battered a few people and them came out looking for more. I mean, a lot of people in them bars had stayed out of the way because you really thought that O'Reilly's was all the coppers were interested in. But in the end they were hitting people who had just been sitting having a beer at a bar well away from it. We'd tried to sort of step back out the way, hoping the Old Bill would steam past and ignore us, but once they'd gone by we tried to walk our way out and ended up doing a runner ourselves because they came back looking for seconds. It was mental. We had to run right through the coppers who'd gone down the road first of all. Fuck knows how we got through. I saw this one lad lying on the deck who'd been clubbed and he was pissing blood. People were trying to get to him, but the coppers were standing over him holding up their truncheons and shields threatening to whack anyone who came close. These other coppers arrived and tried to pick him up and drag him back up but he was out of it, totally shot. Some geezer was shouting at the coppers to leave him still and get some help, but when he started to move towards him this copper ran forward and booted him to keep him off.

Back up the road you could see it had kicked off. People were coming down holding their heads. There were loads of people with blood all over them. I mean it was really naughty, difficult to describe, but I just wanted to get out. It was way too much for me to keep hanging around anyway, but then you get a few hundred yards up the road and it's like nothing happened! People are still eating and drinking. Weird! You can still hear all the sirens and the noise, and all the people in the bars are looking at everyone running past covered in blood thinking, 'What the fuck!' It's like another world.

People were going mental about the coppers but everywhere you looked they had got themselves geared up, and after seeing what they had done I wouldn't go near one of those bastards. There were a few lads going mental at them, but they would just draw the truncheon and club them, no messing around.

At this stage my mate and me are thinking, 'Let's just get back to the hotel, hook up with the others, keep out the way and have a drink there'. Because you know sooner or later it's going to kick off wherever you end up. I didn't fancy hanging around the bars because you never know, some plain-clothes copper might see you, remember your face and put two and two together, come up with five and you're nicked! The thing was, our hotel was up near the station, which is where all the Turks and Arabs live, so getting back up there was a nightmare. Everyone you saw you thought was going to stab you. In the end we got back all right at around 9.30 p.m. There were a few other England lads staying in the hotel that we'd met earlier, and they were saying that after what they'd seen they might just head back home first thing in the morning. They didn't have tickets for the game anyway. The rest of our lot didn't get back until after 11.30 p.m. They said the coppers were just rounding people up and battering them. All they had been doing was trying to keep out of the way, but the Turks and Arabs were out in groups picking up people who'd got separated and giving them a hiding, so they had ended up having to go all the way out to the airport before they could find a cab that would bring them back to the hotel.

This incident was said to have been provoked by abusive comments shouted at a local Moroccan woman as she had passed by the bar. The woman allegedly returned to her home very distressed, which led to a group of locals getting a mob together and heading back down towards O'Reilly's bar to confront the English fans. Whether or not those allegations are true we'll never know, but it should also be pointed out that reportedly the local population had been inciting the English fans for most of the day and that their provocation had for the most part gone unchecked by the police. Prior to the tournament's kick-off, much had been made of the Belgian police and their stance of 'zero-tolerance'. However, the confrontations which occurred earlier in the tournament and involving both Belgian and Turkish hooligans led many English fans to believe that, as was the case in France 98, this police posturing and pre-tournament hype had already proved to be nothing but empty threats. How wrong they were. O'Reilly's bar had played host to the England fans all day and became a focal point for English fans as well as for the local Turkish population. The strong beer available in Belgium must also have played a part in fuelling the violence, and yet it was interesting to see during a subsequent television interview a representative of O'Reilly's, pouring righteous scorn on the English fans in his bar, many of whom he believed had come just to cause trouble. Surely if that had truly been the case, a more decent act would have been to shut up shop instead of filling his tills with money. Indeed, had the Belgian police taken a lesson from their Dutch counterparts and closed any bar where the likelihood of trouble loomed, this whole incident could well have been prevented rather than provoked.

* * *

Suddenly the streets of Belgium's capital had become a battleground, and in the ensuing war there was only ever going to be one winner as the Belgian riot police took on anyone who got in their way. P.N. of Reading is one of the many innocent fans who got caught up in the chaos;

While I was sitting in the cells waiting to be deported all I could think of was my wife, her parents, our kid and my job. What the hell were they going to make of the news that I had been deported? One of the scum, a football hooligan? I've got a battle on my hands now, a battle in which my solicitor reckons he has little if any chance of clearing my name. But I am going to fight it all the way just to prove to my wife and both our parents that I wasn't involved, that I did everything to stay out of the way and that I am not a football hooligan. The only thing that turned in my favour was that they didn't formally arrest me. That way I can keep the whole incident secret from my work, although I live in fear of someone spilling the beans and telling one of my bosses; you know what people can be like. They all knew I was going out and so now I am living a lie having told them that I just stayed in my hotel once the trouble had started and watched the game on telly.

You could see there was going to be trouble. There were drunken English lads all over the place singing offensive songs, being abusive, all the stuff you hate about the English abroad. But there were so many police around that you thought they could keep it all under control and manage to weed out the real trouble-makers from the true fans. We were sitting outside a bar just drinking and taking in the atmosphere. We'd eaten there, the bar staff were friendly and it was great. Everyone there was just out for a good night. There were no hooligans, just genuine fans – all small groups of people, no mob or anything like that. Then all hell broke loose. You could hear the noise come from up the road and a few lads in the bar jumped up to see what was happening.

Suddenly we realised it'd all gone off and so like most of the people around us we picked up our beer and moved inside the bar to keep out the way. The owner of this bar was a really nice guy, a *really* nice guy. I felt so sorry for him. We'd been talking to him on and off for most of the afternoon. He went out to see what was happening and then quickly started to tell everyone left outside to get in as people were running down the road towards us. Then a load went running past and some ran into the bar in order to get out of the way. I don't know if they were hooligans or not, I've no idea, but the police came down the road behind them and just chased in after them. They knocked tables over, chairs . . . it was chaos in there. One lad got hit over the head with a baton. Like I say, he might have been causing trouble – I don't know – but he was bleeding really badly.

The police then moved back outside. People were really genuinely scared, and shouting, and then just when it looked like calming down the police went and fired tear gas right into the bar. I've never experienced anything like it. It burns your throat like nothing else and has you choking in seconds. It's really frightening. You just can't breath. All you want is to get some fresh air in your lungs. There were people pushing over each other to get outside; it was terrible. My little girl suffers from asthma. If she had've been in there I am certain she would have choked to death! They could have killed someone for all they knew. There were all sorts of people in that bar; they didn't know who or what was in there.

By the time I got outside I could hardly stand, but all of a sudden I got hit across the back by something and then found myself being dragged away by four or five police-men. They got me face-down on the floor. One of them was pushing my face against the pavement and I got kicked in the ribs four or five times. That was making it even harder to breathe and I was in a real panic. They grabbed my hands behind my back and then I felt this thing tighten around my wrists. They pulled it really tight and then lifted me to my feet and ran me off down the street. There were cameramen taking pictures and filming everything. It was like some nightmare. I was thinking, 'This can't be happening. Not to me! I've done nothing wrong.'

They then took me into this street that they had put barriers across. There were loads of other English fans there, all sitting down in rows. They stood me up against a wall, went through my pockets and then put me in one of the rows behind this other lad. It was really frightening. The police were so fired up. Some of them were walking down the rows and just kicking anyone. They looked like they were enjoying it. Others were laughing at us and calling us English scum; it was total humiliation. A few minutes later they brought my friend into the street as well, but the other two lads we were with somehow managed to get away – although we didn't know that at the time. My mate is a lovely bloke. He wouldn't say boo to a goose now, but when he was younger he got arrested at football after a fight with Cardiff at Elm Park. That was over twenty years ago; he's thirty-nine years old now, a family man. He's got a good job, a lovely wife and three kids, but once they check his record he'll probably be banned for life. He isn't a hooligan – he's a grown man now, not a young lad!

They kept us there for about three hours. It was freezing. They just kept bringing more and more lads in; all of them were saying the same thing – that the police were just out to arrest anybody who was English. Eventually they started taking us away in vans and off to the cells. As they put us in the vans there were all these locals watching and they were jeering and applauding the police.

They took us to these cells, which were terrible. The only food they gave us was cake – that and warm water – which tasted disgusting. They took my name, and my passport, although they gave that back to me in the end. We weren't allowed to speak to anyone like a solicitor, although I wasn't about to risk upsetting them by asking for one anyway. Most people in there were really disgusted with the way we were treated. They never told us if we were going to be charged or anything. I know that there must have been a few lads in there. There were some who seemed to know what was going to happen to us as they just sat it out, saying we'd all just get deported. They didn't seem bothered, but most of the blokes I spoke to swore they were innocent like me. They held us for hours. I had no chance of phoning my wife and I knew she would have been scared out of her wits at me not ringing. I always ring her every day no matter where I am – whether I am working or away fishing with my mates, wherever. Eventually my friend and I got put on a plane and flown back to Stanstead Airport. I still couldn't believe this was happening. Again, all the cameras were there to take pictures, and the amount of police waiting for our arrival . . . it was like something out of an old war-film.

When I rang my wife I felt so ashamed. Even though I'd done nothing wrong I felt ashamed. She burst into tears straightaway but she believes me, she knows I wouldn't get involved in anything like that. But for her sake and mine I really feel I have to clear my name. I don't know if anyone else who got deported is doing the same thing or not, but I really feel there should be something set up for people like me and all the others who had the same thing happen to them. They said the same thing happened to English fans in Italy and in France, but you don't believe it unless you experience it yourself. I never expected it to happen to me – never. The bruises I had when I got back! I took a load of pictures, but again my solicitor says it's going to be hard to prove it was the police who did it. How am I going to track down the ones who arrested me? I've got no chance. The Belgians will just deny everything and say it was probably Turks who did it to me, not them.

* * *

Sporadic incidents of violence broke out well into the early hours of the following morning, many stoked up by the news that one English fan had been stabbed and was seriously ill in hospital. All in all, more than 350 English fans were rounded up and deported following the violence that occurred in Brussels that night, and yet from that number only two were charged with any offence as the Belgian authorities' policy of zero-tolerance appeared to be directed purely towards the English. The Belgian police appeared unrepentant as their official police spokesman, Christian De Coninck, declared to one news reporter that he felt his force should have detained and deported the English in even greater numbers. It was almost as if the Belgian police had been waiting for this moment to arrive, because to many they appeared to be given free rein to seek out anyone wearing the red, white and blue of England and hopefully send a message across the water at the same time. The only trouble being that that message came far too late, as by this time the violence had already spread. Mickey from Essex gives his version of what went on down in Charleroi:

> We were up in the town square when it all kicked off. It had been brewing up all day. There were plenty of riot police around, but so what? They just sat back until it all went off anyway. You had everyone up there: Germans, Turks and then a load of French turned up – that's when it all started to happen. Up until then, the Turks had just been driving around and sussing everything out. The English and Germans had just been mouthing off at each other, getting pissed and singing. Then a few carloads of frogs turned up and they were driving around making a right racket because they had just won their match. It really wound everyone up after a while. They're blasting out on their car horns and shouting fuck knows what. Some lad then lobs a glass at this motor, and of course once one's gone a few more follow, don't they? Well what the fuck do they expect? Fancy going out and giving a mob

of pissed-up England fans the large! What the fuck were they doing in Charleroi anyway? Why didn't they just fuck off back to France?

All of a sudden the old buzz has gone around the bar. The verbal towards the Germans got a bit louder and all the other bars joined in the singing. Then this car came around, full of Turks shouting out of the windows, and of course they got the same treatment as the Froggies got. A couple of minutes later this Turk bloke comes up to the bar, all on his own, tooled up, and just clumps this lad over the head with something or other! Someone said later it was a car jack. Mad fucker! Anyway, this lad's gone down, but his mate chases the Turk off up the road like some scared rabbit. So it's like, 'Here we go. Any minute now and it's going to go off big-time.' Then, sure enough, word's gone round that we're going to have it away with the Krauts. Then the shout goes up and we steam into them. All that mouth and then they're straight on their toes. It's lovely that, though, that feeling of taking a place over. We owned the square then – it was ours. It's like you've made a little bit of England in a foreign country, lovely. What a buzz that is.

Course, then the Old Bill decide to put on a show by bringing out the riot gear and giving it some. We're just winding them up. Singing at the top of our voices 'Rule Britannia' and taking the piss – lovely! Take that uniform off and they're wankers. There's hundreds of them all tooled up. Water cannons, the lot, and what have we got? Fuck all but a few bottles to lob at them! But we'll still have a go, won't we, still put on a show. That's the bulldog spirit for you; that's why they hate us so much. They envy what we've got inside, that spirit in our blood that makes us English.

The incident described above and involving the Turkish fan hitting the English lad gives a useful insight to the stance taken by the British press reporting on the violence that erupted during Euro 2000. The episode was caught in its entirety on camera, and the original TV footage shown here did indeed include pictures of an aggressive Turkish hooligan brandishing a piece of metal and threatening the English fans standing outside that bar. However, this footage was later cut back to show nothing more than the subsequent retaliation of an English lad chasing the Turk up the road. The clip has on numerous news items and documentaries been cited as evidence of the English scum abroad, and yet thanks to a clever piece of editing it fails to represent the complete picture. While filing a report on the trouble for the *Trevor McDonald Tonight* programme, news correspondent Mark Austin introduced his own piece thus: 'This is our take on the violence.' It is easy for Joe Public to look at those pictures now and experience feelings of utter disgust. I don't deny for one minute that it looks ugly and that it is shameful. But is it really so surprising that someone reacted in such a way, having just seeing their friend get hit on the head with a piece of metal while the police stood back and did nothing?

During the night sporadic outbreaks of violence continued on the streets of Charleroi as the police moved in to close bars and disperse the mobs. More than 170 English fans were held overnight under what the police described as 'preventative arrests'. The following day all were deported without charge.

The most brutal attack in Charleroi that night came at just after 1.20 a.m. and took place in what was by this time a relatively quiet main square. As a group of English fans drank in Le Tonneau bar, a car suddenly screeched to a halt outside and three Turks jumped out. They then ran fowards the bar, shouting and gesturing towards those inside. One of the three ran forward and stabbed an English fan in the chest before heading back to the car and disappearing into the night. This was yet another totally unprovoked attack, and it resulted in a man lying critically ill in hospital. It also provided clear indication that still more violence was sure to follow.

19

Brussels Sprouts Violence

Saturday 17 June 2000

At four o'clock in the morning the wife is driving me to the train station when news comes across the radio that an England fan has been stabbed in Belgium. The wife looks at me and asks, 'Are we turning back, then?'

I lean forward and switch the radio off. It's not the best news with which to start the day. As we say our goodbyes my wife looks worried while I try to look confident and calm. Inside I am shitting a brick. I've got no match ticket and, to be honest, I've probably got more chance of waking up with Billie Piper sitting on my face than I have of getting one. I am travelling alone, people are getting stabbed, and there's a morgue set up in case I get killed. What the hell am I doing? I try to stay calm by reminding myself that by this time tomorrow I'll be back in England again – hopefully!

As I travel the tube to Waterloo, I'm confronted with the reality that I have quite literally turned into a complete coward when I bump into a young girl and her mother. The girl is no older than fifteen and is decked out in the full England gear; a signed shirt, a scarf tied to her coat and baseball cap on her head. She is grinning from ear to ear, exposing her metal-braced teeth and looking more excited than a teletubby on acid. I can't help but ask the most obvious question: 'Are you off to the football?'

'Yes. I can't believe it – I only got to hear I was going on Wednesday.'

I feel like grabbing hold of her and shaking her while offering the advice I am sure she needs to hear: 'Don't go – you'll get killed.' I resist the temptation, though a quick glance at her mother tells me that she too fears the same outcome. Oh, what it must be like to be that young and naïve.

I arrive at Waterloo to find police scouring the concourse looking for known faces and checking people's tickets and passports. I slip my ticket into the barrier and manage to walk through unchallenged. At 6.14 a.m. my EuroStar train slowly pulls out of the station and I head for the buffet-car where I find a mix of lads and Transport Police. As the train rolls through Vauxhall I realise that we're travelling directly above one of my favourite nightclubs, namely Cloud 9. A look at my watch tells me that on most Saturday mornings at this time I'd be just about leaving the place, having enjoyed the rush of a top all-nighter instead of trundling over the top of it on my way to World War Three. Service begins in the buffet-car at 6.25 a.m. and to my amazement the first lad in the queue places the following order; 'Twelve cans of Kronenburg please, love.'

Even the coppers laugh and shake their heads. However, their humour is somewhat subdued when the next three lads place similar orders and the penny drops that for them this is going to be one long day.

Soon into the journey I get chatting to three lads, two of whom follow Chelsea while the other has been forced into following a local Saturday side called Bocca Seniors because going to top-class football is out of his price-range. Still, his commitment to the club can't be denied as he goes on to tell everyone and anyone that the mighty Bocca are in fact of such class that, rather than predict how many they will win by each week, they just ask the opposition by how many they would like to get beaten! (A scenario I feel rather reminiscent of the situation

Glasgow Rangers have had over their opposition up in Scotland prior to this season!) The group are all members of the England Members' Club and proud to tell me that they have tickets for every game: there aren't too many people around who have clocked up more points on their travels with the national team than they have. At 7.00 a.m. they offer me my first beer of the day, and despite my earlier disbelief that people could even contemplate drinking at such an hour, I now feel it would be rude to decline their hospitality and so join the masses. Although there's some discussion about whether or not we should be drinking this particular brand of German beer on such an historic day. The Bocca fan is actually on an early-morning-drinks ban. Apparently, a year or so back he had a bang on the head and consequently gets drunk far too rapidly for his own and everybody else's safety. In fact, after getting steamed up at the Eindhoven match he had got a bit lippy with the police, who then pulled over the group and began checking their passports – since when Bocca Boy had not seen his England Members' Club card. The worrying thing for him now is that he may well find himself banned when he applies for any England tickets in the future.

On arriving in Brussels, the three of them are picking up a hire-car and staying out until after the Romania fixture. Like me, they have heard about last night's trouble, so they've decided to find a small town a few miles outside of Charleroi rather than heading straight into the melting pot. They are also hooking up with a couple of Swedish guys they met when following England to Scandinavia a few years back. They tell me that as well as following their own national team, the Swedes love watching England because of the atmosphere the supporters generate. The lads also kindly offer me the chance of joining them – I must appear to be a bit of a Billy-No-Mates travelling alone, and as I think their offer is one made more out of pity than anything else none of us mentions it again.

Also on the train are a few West Ham fans travelling with a lad from Blackburn. It turns out that one of the Londoners works the markets and has a stall every Saturday at the Bovingdon

Airfield just a few miles from where I live. I mention this because the Airfield backs up to the local prison, known as The Mount, a so-called secure unit with a dramatic history for outlandish escapes. One example of such was the time when two inmates were being given a course in bricklaying and were left alone with one tutor, a spade, some bricks and a whole lot of scaffolding . . . No, it doesn't take a genius, does it! The other Londoner goes on to tell me that while his brother was detained at The Mount he would turn up at the market stall every Saturday and have a cup of coffee before re-entering the prison, stacked up with that week's 'orders'! One week he even came out carrying the video recorder he had just 'borrowed' from the guards' room in the hope of offloading it to some unsuspecting Saturday-morning punter!

One lad then starts telling everyone that the German police have apparently rounded up and jailed nearly all of their top-category hooligans in a massive crackdown to prevent them from travelling and causing trouble with the English and Turks. But unlike most of the rumours spread among the English travelling fans, this one actually turns out to be true. In an unprecedented measure, the German government had passed regulations allowing the police to move in on known troublemakers and restrict them from leaving their country. All in all, 290 known German hooligans had their freedom to travel removed, while a further 195 were instructed to report to the local authorities prior to kick-off of any of Germany's games. This was a brave move by the German government, and one which demonstrates that some countries, rather than hold ill-informed television debates and parliamentary sessions, actually believe that actions often speak louder than words.

At 10.02 a.m. the train pulls to a stop in Brussels and the England fans pile on to the platform and begin queuing at the passport-checking desks. This is a scene far removed from the one I witnessed at Eindhoven. Here there is no singing, no 'ING-GER-LAND' greeting our arrival, just the muttering of nervous fans eager to get away from the eyes of the police so they can either catch a connection directly to Charleroi or head off into

Brussels and find their hotels. As the queue moves forward I suddenly hear a guy doing the best John Barnes impression I've ever experienced, only to look round and see that it is in fact the very man himself, standing right there behind me. Being a Watford fan I just couldn't help myself: 'Mr Barnes, as a Hornet I'd like to tell you you're the best player I've ever seen pull on the shirt.'

His reply: 'Yeah, yeah. You've told me before.'

He doesn't even have the decency to look me in the eye. What does he *mean*, I'd told him before? I had paid the man my ultimate compliment. I had travelled the country to watch him play and in support of the Watford team that made his career. And here he is talking to me like I'm just a piece of shit. As I take the escalator down, the guy next to me pipes up: 'He's always been arrogant, Barnes has.' The lad's support buoys me up.

'What a self-centred wanker, eh? Anyway, Blissett was always better than him.' A short pause and then the final pay-off, just to make me feel better; 'Never did it for England, did he, eh?'

The incident reminds me why I've never been one for idolising players. I suddenly have a flashback to 1978 when I was standing on the hard shoulder of the M1 motorway after our coach had broken down in a traffic-jam on the way home from a 4–2 win at Walsall. The players' bus then went past, and as we ran out to applaud them they didn't truly acknowledge our support – just like Barnes didn't a few moments back. My brother who I was with at the time never set foot inside Vicarage Road again, and went on to commit the cardinal sin of supporting the team up the road and WFC's fiercest rival: L*t*n. I would like to add that, thankfully, that brother of mine is now cured of that particular illness, but he still hates Watford more than any other side in the country – bar Bristol City, of course!

After hanging around the station for a few moments, the rumour begins to circulate that the Belgian police in Charleroi have already deported some 300 England fans. I decide it's probably best to spend a few hours in Brussels and see for myself whether or not the situation described on the early morning radio is half as bad as they made out. Immediately I leave the station I find myself wandering down a maze of side-streets where many of the shop-signs are written in Arabic and the vast majority of people appear to be of either Eastern European or Arabic origin. I'm getting a few dodgy looks from the locals and suddenly feel that this is not the right place for a lone England fan to be, so I turn tail and retrace my tracks in the hope of finding somewhere that feels a little less threatening.

As I make my way towards the city centre, the sun beats down and I notice that each bar I pass has greater numbers of Englishmen drinking outside it. Also as I walk I get talking to a group of lads from Huddersfield who, like me, have only just arrived in the city; they're now off to meet some mates who were staying in town last night. The report is that things were sporadically kicking off all over the place and that the majority of the trouble for England fans was with the police rather than the Turks. Now, once in the centre of town, English fans are out in extraordinary numbers, every bar crammed to the nines with bare-chested fans soaking up both the sun and the strong local brew. It's amazing to see how many England fans have travelled over the water, most of them in groups of three or four but interspersed among them big mobs who it appears have taken over entire bars and made them their own. Though visible, the police are by and large keeping a low profile and the general mood seems to be one of happy calm – not the chaos I had expected to find. After wandering about for an hour or so, I finally sit myself down in a bar situated on the main drag leading back up to the station. Opposite me is a small square and to the side a large church. As ever when you travel with England, it's, only a matter of minutes before I've got myself a whole new bunch of drinking-partners.

In the bar around me are lads from Tamworth, Barnet, Brighton and Peterborough, none of whom I had met before, but who are now getting on like old mates. This is what makes travelling away with the national team so worthwhile. Despite all my reservations and worries, deep down I knew it would end up like this – like it always does – lads just coming together, sharing stories and looking out for one another. It's top-drawer and something I'll always love being a part of, being Englishmen abroad. I end up talking with Jason, one of the lads from Tamworth, who's a supporter of Stoke City. He tells me that the last night had been well naughty and points to a lad sitting a few tables back from us with his head wrapped in bandages. We call him over and he goes on to tell us just what happened:

We hadn't been here long, just a few hours. I'd come out with some other lads, all of us Peterborough. We were sitting just over the road there, kind of keeping out the way, when it all kicked off. You could tell it was going to go but like I say, we were over that side. Then the police went mental and just battered anyone. You know what it's like, everyone starts running and so you go to get out of the way. And then suddenly I was down. A copper must have come up behind me and done it. Right on the side of the head, he got me. I didn't even see it coming – or who did it. The next thing I know I am getting dragged along by two cops and thrown into a van with blood pouring down my face. I've got no idea what's happened to the rest of the lads. I haven't seen any of them since. The police took me straight to the hospital. I think they were worried about the amount of blood I was losing, but when they got me there they refused to stitch me up unless I paid £200 a stitch, or something. I don't really remember; they were after money anyway, but I didn't have any on me. I just wanted to get out of there and get away from the coppers. I've got nothing on me now. My wallets' gone, my ticket home. I've got nothing. They must have had it away. My money, everything! We were meant to be meeting some bloke who said he had tickets outside that burger bar at two o'clock today. I am hoping my mates turn up otherwise I am on my own. I've no idea what's happened to them.

The truth is that the lad is shot to pieces. His eyes look glazed over and he didn't really appear to be 100 per cent sure of what's going on around him. The amount of blood he must have lost is unthinkable. His white Lacoste\shirt and cream Stone Island jacket are now matted red, as are the bandages wrapped around his wound. He looks like some kind of war veteran rather than a lad out to watch a football match. I reckon if a press photographer had passed, us by, then tomorrow under the banner 'THE FACE OF ENGLISH FOOTBALL VIOLENCE' this lad's face will surely fill the front page of every tabloid and broadsheet throughout Europe. They'd never stop to ask the true story behind the lad's predicament, let alone print it. This is a bizarre scene: lads sitting in a bar, happily drinking, one of their crowd casually unaware of the fact his head appeared to have just exploded. As the public walked by, many stopped and stared, both shocked and amazed that someone should be casually sitting in a bar looking as he did with a beer in his hand. It was clear to the rest of us that the lad needed serious medical attention, but he was having none of it. All he wanted to do was hook up with his mates, make sure they were all right and then get himself home so that he could get his head treated back in England. But as the hours passed it was clear that his mates were never going to show, the most likely outcome of their evening being that the police had already seen them safely back across the Channel.

A group of pissed-up lads soon appeared outside the bar carrying a Stoke City flag and singing to their heart's content. Suddenly the bar owner appeared to be looking more than a little worried, but the sight of two policemen keeping both a watchful eye and discreet distance soon calmed his nerves. One of the lads then draped the flag over a signpost, at which Jason spoke up: 'Ah, I know him. He's from Tamworth he is. He ain't Stoke, he's fucking Wolves!' He called the lad over. 'All right? What you doing with the Stoke lads?'

'We've been having the right crack. Last night we were well at it with the coppers, and we've been winding 'em up today an' all. Don't tell that lot I am Wolves, they'll fucking kill me. Tonight's going to be mental here.'

The lad was shitfaced, and inside I am thinking: 'Mate, if the Old Bill get hold of you in that state, you're fucked.' But there is no point in sharing my thoughts; he's wrapped up in it all, it's his life and he doesn't give a toss. The thing is there are hundreds of lads like him, pissed up and wandering the streets. To them the events of the night before haven't offered a warning because, unlike some, they have lived to fight and get pissed another day. Not even the sight of the lad from Peterborough sitting there covered in blood stops to make them think. No, they got away with it. They are still there, still giving it some, and they love it. You see, it's all a game, a game I fully understand but thankfully no longer partake in.

The pair of them then go on to tell me about a situation they recently witnessed down at their local pub. It's a story of political correctness clearly gone crazy. The pub in question was once called The Scotsman but following a campaign by a few of the locals it was agreed that it should be renamed The Saint George. However, somewhere along the line a spanner was thrown in the works by someone suggesting to the brewery that the new name for the pub could, in theory, be seen to have racist undertones. Fearful of any adverse publicity, the brewery took a long deep bow to the political correctness movement and began moves to block the name-change, unfortunately underestimating the anger such a U-turn would incite in Jason and his drinking partners. The idea of not being able to honour their own national saint, especially at a time when themed Irish pubs and Scots' nights are deemed the norm in almost every high street, sent the locals mental. The campaign eventually roused so much feeling that the story reached the local television station's evening news, forcing the brewery's hand yet again and resulting in the pub's regulars getting their own way and St George finally standing on the same level as St Patrick and St Andrew. Why some people still see the Cross of St George as a racist symbol I'll never know. England and the vast majority of its people are only too happy to allow other cultures and nationalities the right to display their own banners and celebrate their own saints and gods. Many actively encourage and even partake in those celebrations – I mean, any excuse for a piss-up. So why do the English still have to seek permission, go down on bended knees and almost excuse our own traditions? The do-gooders and right-on groups who raise such issues are usually the first to argue the rights of others – and rightly so in many cases – but surely those rights also extend to those of English origin who happen to shield a love for their own heritage. And yet I can't help but think that for some of these groups, such allegations regarding the actions of the English are merely part of the agenda, because they do nothing but fuel the political fire and highlight the groups' existence. Surely, hinting at such racist undertones gives credence to such rubbish. Left alone, the vast majority of people wouldn't even notice anything of the sort. In fact, I think the people in question need to remind themselves that we live in a democracy and thus each person deserves to have their say as much as anyone else. And that includes the English.

Sitting on a table just a few feet away are a group of lads from Northamptonshire. They're suddenly joined by another lad clutching a copy of an English newspaper, the picture on the front page of which soon has them sitting up and taking notice. It shows one of their mates being tugged away from a crowd of England fans by two plain-clothes coppers, one of whom appears to be hitting out at the bloke's legs with some kind of long truncheon. I have since seen the film footage of this incident many times. The lad had been spotted by police, who deemed him some kind of ringleader and therefore separated him from the mob and dragged him across the road; all the while one of the officers whacked away at his legs like a madman. How the guy managed to stay on his feet I'll never know, but he must have sustained some serious injuries during such a beating. This is the kind of stuff the press long for. It could also ruin the poor bastard's life. The footage of the incident will undoubtedly be repeated on our television screens for years to come, whether or not any of the accusations laid against the lad prove to be upheld: such details will simply fade into insignificance the next time some television editor is looking for the stereotypical image of the English hooligan abroad.

The next table down from us plays host to a load of – dare I say it? – L*t*n T**n fans. I must admit this took me by surprise as at a quick glance they appeared to be quite normal. On hearing such distressing news, I can't help but acknowledge the positive effects the implication of the Care in the Community system has had on the lives of people such as these. A few years back they probably wouldn't have been allowed out of the house unattended, let alone out of the country, and yet here they are, enjoying a window-lickers' outing like some big, happy family of retards. They actually turn out to be a good bunch of lads despite their obvious mental problems. Lads who take great joy in giving me some amusing though obviously misguided verbal abuse. However, one of them receives a rather distressing phonecall from his mates down in Charleroi with the news that, while we've been soaking up the sun in Brussels, all hell was breaking loose down in the south of the country. The English lads had finally got it on with their German counterparts and the rumour is that some 300 England fans have already been arrested.

On hearing the news, most of the lads in the bar decide there and then to stay put in Brussels to watch the game rather than travel south. None of them has tickets anyway and the best price anyone's been offered is £200 – well over the top and way out of everyone's price-range. For me it's a different story. I've got my coach journey back home to hook up with, so have no choice but to head south; and I've only myself to look out for, so I've got to give finding a ticket a go – after all, what have I got to lose? Once again I've made the mistake of getting more pissed than was my intention, so I reckon the time has come to leave Jason and co. behind and head off back to the station. A few hundred yards ahead of me on the main drag are two parked police vans and a group of officers walking to and fro across the road. Not wanting to be stopped and pulled in for being drunk, I cross the road doing my best 'I can walk in a straight line, officer, honest' impression only to see one of the coppers clock me and cross to block my path 'Excuse me, sir, are you English?'

I am thinking, *'What's Belgian for "no"? Quick* . . . I say. 'Yes,' I say. *Doh!*

'Then you shouldn't go up that way. It's not safe for you because there are Turkish boys looking to fight with anyone who is English. If you want to go to the station then go back that way instead, it's much safer.'

What a nice man, I'm thinking. That's the police for you – always there when you need them. I suddenly realise that this is the very area I was walking around earlier today when I had first arrived in the city, so heed his words and head back from whence I came. As I make my way back through the city centre, I once again pass all the bars full of English fans drinking and can't help but wonder what they would make of the news that the Turks are out and about looking for action again – and just how long it will be until the two groups meet face to face.

As I enter the station a group of about ten lads passes by, heading in the opposite direction. Clocking that they're obviously English, I take the chance to ask them what I personally consider to be a rather innocent question: 'Excuse me, lads, do you know when the next train to Charleroi is due to leave?'

Now surely you'll agree that is not too offensive, but one lad, a short, right hard-looking, shaven-headed meathead turns on me like I'd just asked if he wouldn't mind me shagging his dog. 'You what? Bristol City's 'ere. City's 'ere. Who wants it, eh? City's 'ere – Bristol City!'

I thought he was going to rip my head off. *'Woo there, tiger, easy.'* The rest of the group are like a bunch of bloody meerkats, their heads all popping up and looking around. 'It's all right, mate, I'm English an' all,' I say.

'Yeah well, so what? You want a train? Well there's the fuckin' station, ain't it.'

I tell you what: I wouldn't like to meet this lot when they're upset. I know Bristol City have always had a top firm, but if they've got another five of him then they must be a match for anyone. He looks like one nasty bastard. Incidentally, if you are that lad and you happen to be reading this, may I just say that if I upset you in any way then I really am very, very sorry indeed, OK?

I make my way down on to the packed platform and join hundreds of my countrymen singing their hearts out. The noise is deafening but beautiful. Meanwhile, as we wait to board the train for the forty-minute journey south, some of the English fans already at our destination are enjoying a completely different kind of buzz. My next correspondent is Spanner from the Peoples' Republic of Yorkshire:

> I've never seen so many English lads out. It were fucking top. The Germans never stood a chance; they only had about seventy lads anyway. It were pathetic. Just a load of mouthy twats. I know they said they had stopped all their main lads from travelling, but they could have put on a better show than that.
>
> The whole thing had been warming up over a good few hours. The German lads were being well loud, giving off the Nazi salute an' all that. And so we were having a go back, giving it the *Dambusters* tune, arms out wide, magic. Well funny, that. The police just stood over in one corner and waited. They just let us get on with it. If they'd have put a line of coppers in the middle of the square then they could have stopped anything before it even started. I think the coppers wanted it to go off. You could see they were just waiting for it to start and when they moved the water cannon in, it kind of gave the game away. I noticed they lined the thing up pointing at us, though, rather than at the Germans. All the camera crews were there an' all, bastards. There were more of them than there were coppers for most of the morning. All pointing at us, of course. One thing that always makes me laugh is that you get loads of people just watching and waiting for it to go off. Like

tourists. And they're sitting around drinking right in the middle of where it's obviously going to all go off! And when it happens it's like, 'oh fuck!' The thing was it were the German lads who went for it first. No one says that on the news, do they? It took a few lads by surprise, that, I think, but once they had thrown their bottles they were fucked. They were never up for a fight, they never had the numbers, really, and as soon as we steamed in they fucked right off. They came back about half an hour later, though, once the police had moved in. They then did the same thing again: threw a few bottles and then legged it.

Really it were nothing with them, just a quick charge and that were it. All over in a couple of minutes. But the thing was we done the Germans, which is what it were all about. That's what we'd come out to do, run them and then the Turks. They've still never got close to doing England. That's England for you. We're always there, we'll always turn up, won't we?

Course everyone's buzzing now, and so the police start getting the verbal as well. Another thing. They turned straight on the English, didn't look to me like they did fuck all with the German lads. Just let them run, even though they made the first move. They don't care – all they want is a go with the English. After we'd fucked the Germans off, I moved back out the way 'cause the water cannon moved round and the police got right up for it. Some English lads, though, you've got to give it 'em – they don't give a toss. They started throwing chairs and bottles at the water cannon. As though a plastic chair is going to do anything! The thing is, though, that they're doing it. They're showing the police they don't give a fuck. They put themselves right on the front line for their country. They don't mind getting the odd clump or boot up the arse. Course, no one wants to get arrested, but if you do all you'll have in the morning at worst is a few bruises and a free ticket home.

When that water cannon went off it were hysterical,

people were knocked flying! I never realised how powerful those things were. But it were pointless as it were just taking out anyone. There was this poor sod, just some normal bloke walking around, who had his legs taken right from under him. It were cracking. Then the police steamed forward and started hitting out at anyone who got in the way. People who were nothing to do with it, just looking on, like, then suddenly they're getting hit and pulled over. We shot off down this side-road heading away from the ground and within about 200 yards it were like nothing had ever happened, calm as you like. We were roaring. As we were going though we see this lad smack this cameraman. A right fucking crack it was. Cunt were taking photos of English lads who were all soaked up and that. The whole thing were a great crack and I was there: I was one of the lads who ran Germany at Euro 2000! That'll look nice on the old CV, that will.

The violence predicted by so many was now being met with the full force of the Belgian authorities – an estimated 140 fans were arrested and detained in the single hour between 2.00 p.m. and 3.00 p.m.! As ever with football hooliganism, however, one lad's tale is another lad's lie, and so included below are the contents of an e-mail I found posted up on a rather well-known site. It was addressed to England fans everywhere and had me shaking in my boots:

England, your time is over. You are not the top hooligans in Europe, not even near the top. Galatasaray showed you that. In Charleroi you outnumbered us. You knew all our top boys were stopped from coming and still you didn't want to fight us. We had Bayern, Stuttgart and Hamburg waiting for you, but you had no boys wanting to fight but just throw bottles and chairs. There were no police but you still didn't come at us. All day we stayed and waited. We wanted to fight with you to prove who is best. We wanted to fight for our country no matter how many of you there were, but all you do is shout and throw beer bottles. You had thousands and we only had a hundred but even then you didn't have what it takes. We got tired of waiting. If we had all our top boys you would have had your shitty English arses kicked! Germany laughs at you. See you again soon!

Go on admit it, you're scared!

20

Thank You, God, It Was
Nice Meeting You

The train down to Charleroi is crammed, hot and sweaty. Sitting opposite me is a lad so drunk he can't even speak. He is massive, with hands like bunches of bananas and a look on his face that suggests he's just stepped off the Sunshine bus. Suddenly his head flops forward and for the next few minutes I have to view dribble pouring from the corner of his mouth and soaking his light-blue T-shirt. The young lad sitting next to him is obviously not a friend, and when Drunken Lad's head slumps to one side and begins to use the younger lad as a pillow I just can't resist the temptation: 'Looks like you've pulled, mate! Imagine waking up with him sitting on your face!'

He gives a nervous laugh, checks his watch, sighs and stares out of the window. 'Don't worry, mate, we'll be there in forty-five minutes!'

The train pulls into Charleroi, the English spill out and once again announce their arrival. As ever the singing is loud, but many have their eyes on the rows of riot police lining the subway and guiding us out of the station. Re-emerging into the sunlight, the English are greeted by yet more police, some of whom start pulling people over and checking their passports. So I stay on the outside, avoid any eye-contact and shift past unnoticed. It later transpires that many of the English fans arriving by train without match tickets or passports on them were instantly herded into police vans and held captive. Many pleaded that they had left their passports back at their hotels for safety reasons, but their excuses fell on deaf ears, as the following day they found themselves among the large numbers being deported back to England.

As I make my way into the city centre I notice the number of England fans growing with each passing street. The buzz in the air is electric, the constant hum interspersed by the sound of the odd bottle being smashed against the floor. Amazingly there appears to be even more English here than were present in Eindhoven, something I wouldn't have thought possible. In order to counter the invasion, the Belgian police have turned out in force, deploying 3000 officers on foot and a further 120 on horseback. Added to their number are thirteen water cannons, forty-five dog-handlers and a helicopter that circles above like a wasp waiting for a victim to target. Welcome to Charleroi!

Slowly but surely the feeling washes over me of being part of it all, belonging, that feeling of being an England fan abroad. Charleroi is a town bursting at the seams. A town that had obviously underestimated the drawing-power such a fixture would prove to have for so many of England's football fans. Why they held this match here I'll never know. It's the equivalent of playing the game in a town like Guildford. England v Germany is and was always going to be the biggest game of this tournament, so why here – a town with less than 200 hotel-beds available and a stadium about as safe as Harold Shipman in an old people's home? Indeed, concerns about safety at the stadium were so great following the addition of an extra upper tier to the main stand that the local fire brigade underwent special Alpine-rescue training in preparation for any possible evacuation that might be needed. This may sound ridiculous but is nonetheless 100 per cent true.

Concerns about this being an appropriate location for today's fixture were raised within hours of the draw being made, but

UEFA and the Euro 2000 organisation committee refused to budge. The stance they took not only angered politicians and fans but also led many to believe that once again English football was being well and truly set up for a tumble. Chelsea Don has his say:

Playing that game in Charleroi was a total fit-up, a fit-up for English football. They played that game there for one reason only and that was to shaft the English because we're on the up again, getting back where we belong. I am not talking about the national side – we're miles behind at international level but that's another argument – I am talking about our club sides. Look what we did last year: Chelsea, Arsenal, Leeds and Man United. We're right back up there at the top again and they hate it. They hate to see our football doing well and so they want to put a lid on it again like they did after Heysel. English football needed a kick up the backside after what happened there. We needed that ban as things had gone too far, but have they ever banned anyone else? What about the Turks, the Dutch or the Italians? They've all had their deaths since then, all of them. In places like Croatia, Bulgaria and Hungary it's like a flashback to the 70s and 80s but they don't get banned, do they? No, it's only ever the English.

The people that run football know that wherever England play thousands will turn up without tickets. We did it in Italy and in France. They know it and yet they play the game in one of the smallest stadiums being used for the tournament! They even had to add an extra tier to the stadium. That ground is only used to holding 22,000 so what genius thought that one up? It's guaranteed that come kick-off the stadium will be full of English fans, most of them having bought their tickets on the black market, so why not just give us more tickets in the first place? When will they learn? England fans will pay almost anything to see the match but why let some arsehole tout profit? They should just sell us the tickets.

Not only that, they play it in a shit-hole of a town down in the arse end of nowhere. Making the England fans travel the length of the country was madness. Having the English travel through Brussels – what a blinding idea that was! A city with a load of Turks living in it, yeah, well done! The best place to play that match had to be Rotterdam. There's a stadium holding 50,000. They could have given England 25,000 tickets, Germany 10,000 and still given away enough freebies to keep all the freeloaders happy. Rotterdam's the biggest port in Europe, the ferry terminal's just up the road. Being that close to the port would have made it so much easier for everyone, the fans and the police. They could have shipped the English in and out within hours and kept them well away from the rest of the country, no problem. Ban drinking on the ferries going both ways and you've got the problem virtually sorted out. You'd think it would be simple really!

You've got a top stadium geared up for big games – Feyenoord play there, for God's sake. They've got massive support and because they have a hooligan problem the police there would be used to dealing with it should anything go off. Handling foreign supporters isn't a problem for them: there have been eight European Cup finals at that ground, four of those involving English clubs. It's all geared up for top games so why didn't they play it there? If they really had to play the game in Belgium then surely they should have done it in Brugge and for exactly the same reasons: it's near the port, a top European side, it's obvious. So what if the Germans had to travel further? They weren't the problem. They were never going to travel in the same numbers as England. I know the stadium is still small there, but it's a much better ground than the one at Charleroi. In fact in many ways Brugge would have been better than Rotterdam. With both Ostende and Zeebrugge near they could have had any troublemakers on a bus and out of there before they knew what had hit them. And all the genuine fans could have been on a ferry and back across the Channel by midnight if they wanted to! Brugge is right up there at the top, the English fans wouldn't have had to travel further than twelve miles from the coast. They could have kept them all up in that little corner of the country, easy.

But no, they had to play it in Charleroi. No one had heard of the place before they made that draw. They make the English travel the length of the country and play the match in a town with no football history, no tradition and nothing to do but drink. They know that England fans get pissed up wherever they go and yet they play the game in Belgium where the beer's extra strong and leave the bars open all day. Everyone knows drinking causes most of the problems. They say other fans drink but don't get violent. So what? This isn't about other fans. The English do drink and play up: accept it and then deal with it.

Games don't come much bigger than England v Germany. It's the war, the World Cup, Euro 96, all that history. We hate each other, we always will! Even the most daft of bastards could have seen that here was a riot waiting to happen. That's why I reckon we were set up. There was not one good reason for playing that game there, not one. It was the worst possible venue and everybody told them so the minute they announced that game. So why did they refuse to listen? Some said it was because they didn't want to be seen as giving into the hooligans, but that's rubbish. By playing that game there they played right into the hands of the hooligans. From day one they said that the problem of containing the hooligans was one of the major priorities of the tournament, but as soon as they were given a problem they did nothing to stop it. I think there are people within UEFA who wanted to see English football as well as the English nation disgraced. They all have problems themselves but want to keep it known as the English disease so as to keep their own noses clean. And you can't tell me that, with the final bidding for the 2006 World Cup just around the corner, there weren't some rubbing their hands at the prospect of

English hooligans going on the rampage and kicking our bid into touch. Only a pillock couldn't see that. We send Bobby Charlton around the world ten times licking peoples' arses while they just wait for Euro 2000 and a few hundred lads to kick off and the job's done for them.

The violence sickens me. Not just because of what those idiots were doing to the reputation of our country and our football, but because I could see them walking right into it. Those pricks have put English football right back on the edge and opened the door for UEFA and FIFA to kick us right back out again. I believe they knew exactly what they were doing by playing that game in Charleroi. On their part it was a clever move as it covered their backs completely, that's why they wouldn't move it. We all know that in an ideal world you should be able to play a football match in any stadium and in any town and that crowd trouble should be a thing of the past. People shouldn't have their lives disrupted or their businesses threatened just because a football match is coming to town. Every rational person knows that. The problem is this isn't an ideal world, is it?

Football violence is still part of football. It comes to town whenever a big tournament or major match takes place and it was the authorities' job to deal with it to the best of their abilities. They owed it to the people of Belgium and Holland and they owed it to all the genuine fans who wanted to travel and watch the games in safety. But they never listened to the fans or the police, all the time believing that they knew best, and then surprise, surprise, when it went wrong they just threw their hands up in disgust and pointed the finger at the English. Well, that's not good enough. They should have done more. They should have moved that game and I think they should shoulder most of the blame for what happened. But sure as shit they won't, and who is there for them to answer to anyway?

All the flack, all the bad press has all been deflected away from them towards the English game. Suddenly we're the scum of Europe again and now the doors open again for them to kick us back out. Brilliant!

I decide that my first task should be to hunt down the coach-park and locate my transport home, and so soaking up the atmosphere, I climb the steep hill towards the Stade Du Pays De Charleroi. Once again the flags line the streets: Leyton Orient, Rotherham, Villa, Bury St Edmunds . . . the whole of England represented. I could wander around and soak this up each and every day of my life, pick a town and then go in search of the flag. Believe me, it wouldn't take long to find it. As I continue my search for the coachpark I discover yet more lack of organisation: not one copper can, or will, point me in the right direction. An hour later when I've found the coach and breathed a sigh of relief, I head off to get pissed. During my search I had spoken to many English lads, all of whom I asked about the prospect of getting a ticket. Although there are supposedly a few on offer, the asking price quoted was never any lower than £200 so I've resigned myself to getting drunk, finding a bar and just wallowing in the atmosphere of being here. In fact I'm not really that bothered because I have all this around me, all this English pride! I've made the effort and, like most of these fans here, that's more than enough for me. Yeah, watching the match back home with my mates would be fun, but it wouldn't be like this – it never could be. There wouldn't be this tension in the air, this underlying threat of the police watching your every move, or the smell of being on foreign soil. England away has the pulse racing, the pride flowing and always, always is slightly tinged with danger.

Behind the end of the stadium that is to play host to the England fans I find a large roundabout decked out with flags, one of which proudly boasts the words 'Watford FC' to which I head over to make my acquaintance. Though the owners of the flag are nowhere to be seen, some fellow Hornets have had the same idea so we sit down and share stories. These lads have tickets for the game but paid big money for them a few weeks prior to coming out. However, one of them hopes to secure an additional ticket for a friend and is busy on the phone trying to track down the tout who is offering up the prize at £250. With little over an hour to go, the lad gives up and we head across the road to find something to eat. On entering the restaurant the first people I see are the Chelsea lads who I met first thing this morning on the EuroStar out.

True to form they offer me yet another free beer and introduce me to their Swedish mates. The lad Bocca looks to have been hitting the sherbets and is now even more animated than he was this morning, while the Swedes look slightly miffed that they've not managed to find a ticket for the match. Suddenly something clicks in my head: what am I doing? In less than an hour England are due to kick-off against Germany and I am standing talking in a restaurant! All right, I know my chances are slim, but I should be busting my nuts trying to hunt down a ticket. I polish off the beer, wish the lads luck and leave them to the pasta.

As I head away from the ground and battle my way through the excited fans strutting in the opposite direction with their tickets safely tucked away, I am filled with envy. Lucky bastards, I hate you! Now the bars are getting full as people eager to secure the best view beer-money can buy. Moving further away from the stadium, I see the glum expressions on the faces of those who weren't able to obtain tickets begin to outnumber the happy, smiling faces of those who were. For a split second the party mood fades and an air of disappointed calm falls on the streets. With less than fifteen minutes to go I convince myself to keep trying. In desperation I take on the demeanour of a sad old wino looking for fag butts as my eyes scan the floor just in case some poor sod has dropped their ticket by mistake.

Finally my heart sinks and I am forced into making an unwanted decision. It's one last walk back up the main drag and, if the worst comes to the worst, I'll find a bar as close to the ground as possible. I turn and head back up the hill, breaking out into a slow jog as I go. The numbers of people out on the pavements are now in the hundreds rather than the thousands that trod here earlier. Darting my way through the crowd, I hear one last pitiful cry going out from a large drunken lad propped up against a car; 'Anyone got a ticket? Please, anyone got a spare ticket? Come on.'

As I run past I flick him a quick glance and out of the corner of my eye notice a man approach him. For some reason the meeting stops me in my tracks. The man is well dressed, wearing a very expensive-looking cream-coloured jacket with dark trousers and looking like he could have just stepped out from a catalogue photo-shoot. He reaches into his jacket pocket, retrieves something from within and then hands it to the lad propped up against the car. The look on the lad's face suddenly changes from desperation to disbelief. I turn and run to the car. 'Excuse me mate, have you got tickets?'

I take him by surprise and he turns to face me. 'Woah, hang on, mate.'

My eyes dart to and fro between his face and the piece of paper now sitting in the other lad's hand. 'You've got tickets. You just sold him a ticket, I saw you do it. Have you got any more and how much?'

The man then places his arm around my shoulder and guides me away from the car. Look, calm down, son, and come with me. Let's just walk up towards the ground and you keep the noise down.' My mind is going mental. I am nearly wetting myself, and he's walking along looking like 007, all calm as you like! 'I tell you what, this is your birthday and Christmas all rolled into one.' He continues, then nudges my hand with his. 'There you are – have that on me!' I look down and see that in his hand he's holding something that looks remarkably like a match ticket! He nudges my hand once more, only this time the words accompanying the gesture have a slightly more urgent edge to them. 'Quick, take it – and enjoy the match!'

I stop dead to inspect the gift. All of a sudden it's as if the sky parts and a single ray of golden light reaches down to illuminate my palm as the realisation hits home that right there, in my greasy little hand, sits a match ticket! I look up but the man is gone. Then it hits me: I've just met God! Well fuck me, I never knew the Almighty dressed so casual!

It *had* to be God, for there could be no other explanation. I'd had a visitation from the one most high. No mere mortal could bear such gifts, surely! Indeed, if that was nothing more than a human, then let me now declare my love for him. I tell you this: I was so happy at that point that were I gay I would have allowed the man to throw me on the floor there and then. He just gave, yes *gave* me a ticket to see England play Germany, for fuck's sake! In fact, I should really go out and bash one out in his honour.

I shake myself back into the real world and run over to the car where the drunken lad's still looking at his ticket in disbelief. His face has the expression of a man who thinks someone is playing a cruel trick and he almost looks as if he is about to throw the ticket away and disregard the whole incident. 'Mate! Mate – did that bloke just give you a ticket?' I ask.

'Well, it looks like one, but . . .'

'*Yes!* He gave me one an' all and they are the real deal. I know what they're like – I had one for Eindhoven – it's genuine.'

For a short moment he sobers up, then we crack up laughing and suddenly we're on our toes towards the ground. The lad's name is Kelvin and he comes from Shrewsbury. Actually, I call him a lad but he must be in his late thirties. He's built like a brick shit-house and as pissed as a fart. We arrive at the top of the hill and I once again check the ticket. The section housing the England fans is marked down as the Blue Sector but our tickets bear the colour red, so I rush to the line of police blocking the road and ask for fresh directions. From behind there's a sudden rush of noise and the expression on the coppers' faces change instantly. I look over my shoulder to witness my first piece of Euro 2000 violence. A few officers move in to break up the scuffle and then from out of the commotion steps a face I know only too well – that of my old mate Wiltshire. He's buzzing. He tells me that he has been playing around with the police all day, as well as the Germans, the local Turks and their North African chums. He has mobbed up with lads from various clubs, northerners and southerners, all for one and all for England. Only now things have turned on them. This particular scuffle is a result of rivalries that really should have been left at home: a lad from Southampton has taken exception to the views expressed by a Portsmouth supporter, Southampton's bitter rivals. One whack later and the Pompey lad's down, cracking his head open on the kerb as he falls.

I tell Wiltshire of my visitation, of the ticket and God, and I search out Kelvin to back up my tale. Kelvin, though, is already on his way. 'Come on, Eddy, let's do the Old Bill.'

What the hell is he doing? I don't believe the lad. He has just been handed a golden egg and all he wants to do is have a dig at some copper. What an idiot. 'Kelvin, you fuckwit. Get back here.'

Thankfully, the moment is short-lived and he returns, buzzing, bouncing, pissed and excited. 'I thought it was going off then. You've got to have it if it goes, eh Eddy?'

He confirms my story for Wiltshire, who can do nothing but shake his head and call me a jammy fucker in return. Yeah, and don't I know it!

With ten minutes to kick-off Kelvin and I are darting back through the side-streets, heading towards the Red Sector of the stadium. As we race up to the metal fencing that marks the first check-point, I glance at the ticket and register the name printed upon it in black ink: EURO 2000 FOUNDATION.

Well, that'll do for me; I could be anyone. Two minutes later I am standing, arms stretched wide, taking in the most beautiful sight: the England and Germany teams lined up down below. I don't believe it – I'm here. And as ever the noise is deafening:

Dud dud. Dud der do dud dud.
Dud dud der der der der der dud dud.
Der der dud dud. Der der der dud dud.
Dud Der Dud dud dud dud der. ENGLAND.

To my left I see the stand housing the England supporters: a mass of colour and movement. Ahead I see the three-tier stand that has caused so much controversy, only now it looks more like an impromptu washing-line, with the Cross-of-St-George flag hanging from every possible vantage point. To my right the colour scheme changes to the yellow, black and red of the German national flag. For a second I convince myself that the Jerries are all really closet Watford fans and are expressing their love for the Hornets by donning the colours that happen to coincide with their national flag. They then shatter the illusion by breaking out into song, and the scene is set.

In Block LX there is no segregation and fans from all over mix excitedly. England v Germany and no segregation! I thankfully discover that I'm sharing my immediate space with some fellow English lads. Pete's from Northampton, and behind us are a group of Nottingham Forest supporters, the flag stretched out across their chests announcing to the world that NFFC are all present and correct. Right behind me sits the makeshift BBC studio, and my joy is complete on witnessing the arrival of the greatest player of all time, Johan Cruyff. Once again the German fans break out in chorus. I am so close I can see their faces, their own national pride etched into their expressions. Around me, almost as one, little groups of English lads rise to the challenge, jumping to their feet and singing right back: 'Who are ya? Who are ya?'

We share the moment by pointing each other out like long-lost friends, exchanging gestures and laughing excitedly. Around us a few Germans are doing their best but they are outnumbered, shouted down. Ten seats down sits the ultimate stereotype: he has the mullet haircut, the leather waistcoat, the faded jeans and a scarf tied around his waist. He stares back at me, the shaven-headed, pissed-up Johnny in his England T-shirt. We exchange our own linguistic unpleasantries, hold the stare for a split second and then laugh at each other. Two fuckwit football supporters sharing the same emotions, both of us caught up in the moment. In truth, he is as much like me as I am like him. Today, we both share the same dream. We both want it just as bad and we are both here for our countries. Sitting halfway between us is another German, only this one is younger and about eight stone lighter. He has the flat-top haircut and small round glasses. He also has the attitude.

* * *

The game kicks off and that familiar brief spell of calm descends upon the crowd. Out on the pitch the England players soon find themselves chasing lost causes and hoofing the ball at every opportunity, while the Germans settle and begin to play with the ball. Not again, surely! From the stand it becomes almost painful to watch, while for some of those outside it was about to get a whole lot worse. D.T. from Suffolk explains:

What happened to us was well out of order. One minute we're in a bar watching the game and the next we're tear gassed, rounded up and marched off. Fucking mad. Someone should be doing something about the way they treated us out there. If it happened over here they would be going spastic. We were up in a bar just off the main square. All the trouble had calmed right down, there were no Germans or Turks around and all everyone was doing was watching the match. There were a few lads out on the street because the bar was so packed, but there was no trouble and most of the coppers had seemed to have done the off. The atmosphere was top, actually, and of course we're having a sing-song and that – well, there was England v Germany on the telly! Then you could hear a few bottles smash and everyone starts looking outside. Rumour spreads that the coppers have turned up again, mob-handed, and that a few lads had been clubbed outside just for singing, so some lads started moving out to see what's going off.

When I get outside I could see that the coppers had us all penned in, so I think, 'For fuck's sake, here we go again!' Then they started to edge forward. As soon as that starts, you know you're in for something so you're not just going to stand there, are you? I mean, all day you've seen lads getting clubbed and arrested for fuck-all, and now they're coming at you. Then bosh, they gas the place. No warning, they just do it. That stuff is lethal, stings like fuck and once you've got it on you or in your lungs, that's it. All hell breaks loose then; chairs and bottles start going. They got hold of a couple of lads and beat the fuck out of them. They just kept whacking away at this lad. Why they're allowed to get away with it I'll never know. There were plenty of TV crews around – one of them must have got what went on at that bar.

They then steamed forward, forced us back inside. No one got out of there. They rounded us up and took us off. No explanation, why or what for. Someone said it was because they wanted all those without tickets hulled in and shipped out. Well, since when has it been against the law to travel without a ticket? If that's the case, then that was wrongful arrest Why isn't the government doing something about that? They held us for over twelve hours before deporting us back home. Twelve hours! They couldn't have wanted us out that quick then, could they? There were lads shipped back with us who had hotel rooms in Brussels where all their gear was just left. One bloke and his mate had gone out by car and he had two mates in at the game as well. They rang him on the mobile afterwards to find out where he was and they're left standing by the car with no way of getting back home! In the end they never even charged us. It's the last time I travel with England away. You tell people you got deported and they think you're scum. They never want to hear or get to know the truth. It's fucking bollocks.

All in all some 300 England fans were detained and deported as a result of incidents such as these following kick-off. Most were held on buses with no toilets and were given nothing more than plastic bags of drinking water for refreshment. Yet while the zero-tolerance policy adopted by the Belgian authorities once again clearly displayed little if any respect for civil liberties, the British media apparently preferred to concentrate on the violence instigated by English hooligans rather than on the abuse of their innocent countrymen's rights.

* * *

At the stadium the England team are going from bad to worse in a display of ineptitude that even has the Germans taking the mickey. They say the Germans have no sense of humour, but when 6000 of them belt out: 'You're shit and you know you are!' even the most ardent English fans around me are forced into a smile. All except Pete, who stands, arms folded, unimpressed: 'Can you imagine the English fans singing a song in another language? Would we bollocks!'

England are so bad I try to disguise my disappointment, telling the lads from Nottingham that if I'd have paid to see this I'd have been well pissed-off. A comment that brings a well-deserved slap to my head.

As half-time draws near, England break forward for what seems like the first time. The ball swings into the box, connects with Michael Owen's head and, before striking the post and bouncing away to safety, sends the German keeper diving to his left. The atmosphere changes immediately. Every English fan jumps to their feet, clutches their head in their hands and bellows out their frustration. The moment shifts the game. Now there is hope, real hope, that England can play, can score. The noise reaches new levels, three sides of the stadium belting out 'Rule Britannia' while the German fans slump to their seats. Now the clock runs faster. Scholes shoots . . . oh so close! The half-time whistle comes. It's 0–0 and England are back in the game.

I spend the interval queuing for non-alcoholic beer and a much-needed piss. Every Englishman is singing, bouncing and loud, while the locals look on with uneasy smiles. You can see they just don't get it, each face bearing the same expression: *'What is it with these crazy English guys? They look so happy and yet feel so threatening!'* An announcement blurts over the PA system: 'A special train is leaving the station at 12.30 a.m. bound for Calais, a nice train on which every Englishman is welcome to travel. Please travel!' The message is greeted with half-hearted-cheers.

As the second half kicks off, I find the path back to my seat blocked so sit in the gangway, four seats down from my bespectacled German flat-head. He doesn't like me jumping to my feet and singing *The Great Escape* theme tune. He hates my arms-out-wide *Dam Busters* song-and-dance number. And as for 'Two World Wars and One World Cup . . . Well, it made *me* laugh. Almost directly below me, David Beckham prepares to swing the ball into the penalty box. He curls his foot around it, sending it spinning towards the goalmouth. It journeys towards Owen. His touch eludes Paul Scholes, takes out the ball-watching German defenders and then arrives at Alan Shearer's head. I swear I can see the whites of his eyes as he picks his spot and sends the ball back across the goal. The keeper remains still, only his head moving as it follows the path of English football history. The side-netting welcomes its prize and the ball nestles down, motionless, safe and secure. Oh my fucking *God!*

'YESSSS! GET IN THERE! YESSSS! YOU DIRTY, ROTTEN, FILTHY GERMAN BASTARDS! YESSSS, HAVE THAT, YOU CUNTS!'

I know it doesn't sound nice, but I've waited, I've waited a long, long time for this moment. Remember Mexico 1970? Remember Italia 90? Euro 96? Well, it's all there, released in that horrible, rotten, heartfelt torrent of abuse. The hurt is at long last on the loose and enjoying its freedom. Someone jumps on my back; Christ knows who it is but he's English and for that I love him. The stadium shakes and down below the hero of the moment, Alan Shearer, pokes his tongue out at the motionless Germans. Behind me an English lad has made the journey from his seat at the back to remind the mullet-haired German of the score, spitting the words into his ear. Disdain, hate and pride forcing every word. The German's stare remains fixed on the green playing-field ahead, although inside he must be fit to explode. My own dancing in the aisle once again upsets my four-eyed German pal. In no uncertain terms he tells me to sit back down while I tell him to shut the fuck up, buoyed by the goal, the atmosphere and the rush of adrenalin that flows through my body. As I begin to edge back to my seat I can't help myself. I ruffle the German's hair, like a dog-handler would that of an obedient pet. 'AAHHHH, YOU GERMAN TOSSER!'

Annoyed, he brushes my hand away while Pete and the lads from Nottingham laugh at a golden moment I'll carry forever. Oh, you lovely German loser!

Now the clock slows. Slows so much that I'd almost swear it stops altogether. The English fans give it their all. Willing the team forward, kicking every ball, caressing every pass. Suddenly we notice that the floodlights above the pitch appear to be moving with the bouncing motion of the English fans away to our left. This brings the questionable safety of the stadium once again to the forefront of my mind, though in truth I do little else for the rest of the game but watch the time slowly, slowly, slowly ebbing away. Then at last the final whistle: 'YESSSSS! YESSSS! YES, FUCK ME, YES!'

It's over; it's 1–0 to the England; we've beaten Germany and the world is a wondrous place. I love my wife, my family, my cat and all my friends. I even love boy-bands at this point. As the Germans head for the exit, their every step is greeted by some Englander or other bellowing a reminder of the score into their ears. The locals also hastily make for the exits, unable to grasp the heady English mixture of joy, anger and relief so openly on show. The announcer again battles to cut through the noise, desperately trying to remind the English fans about the train back to Calais. This time her words are lost beneath a new English song:

> We're not going home,
> We're not going home,
> We're not going, we're not going,
> We're not going home.

The song has some of the locals wincing as the prospect of yet another night of partying and possible violence hits home.

Behind the goal where the England fans are, all you can see is a mass of bouncing red, white and blue. The stand visibly rocks, the lights dart on the pitch but nothing stops the party. It feels dangerous, exciting and alive over there at the moment, while somebody somewhere must be praying that Belgium isn't about to play host to yet another major crowd disaster. Outside, the atmosphere is calmer. People talk loudly but the songs have died down. People move in all directions as they head to the station, the coachpark, their cars and the town square. I run through the streets, arms out wide, shouting at the top of my voice: 'SHEARER, SHEARER, SHEARER!'

No one cares about the happy, mouthy southern twat running around. They have their own feelings of bliss, their own memories and their own tales to tell about the night England finally managed to turn over the Germans. As I head to the coach I somehow bump into two good mates from my home town. First of all there's Steve, who in the old days watched Watford alongside me but later moved over to Chelsea in order to keep getting his kicks. And then a few yards further down the road is Kev, who's always hated violence and is an England Travel Club member and a lifelong Hammers fan. All three of us miles from home but united in the fact that we were actually there to see it with our own eyes. Fucking marvellous!

Waiting by the coach I watch people greet each other like long-lost relatives. The England band march slowly down towards me, while people dance around them like moths would around a flame. A worse band it would be hard to find – they're out of tune and out of time – but it doesn't matter, we all get the point. I board the coach and sit myself down next to a lad from Birmingham who had hoped to have the double seat all to himself for the journey back across the Channel. He tells me that he was in the square and that his son had rung to tell him he had seen him on the news, desperately trying to anchor his beer to the table while the water cannon went about its business. His son had also told him that the violence had looked awful on the television. The reality, my new friend tells me, is that it was nothing much to write home about – just a hundred beered-up lads lobbing bottles and chairs at each other before the police came in and beat the living daylights out of everyone. It's a story I've heard a thousand times and one I've witnessed with my own eyes on numerous occasions.

The *Richard Littlejohn* programme crackles through on the coach radio, the show carried across the Channel and bringing us the usual rubbish. Already there are people moaning back home. They think the team played badly; that Keegan is not the man for the job; and that England were lucky. Are some people *never* happy? Only one thing mattered tonight and that was the result. England needed to win, had to win. We needed to beat the Germans and we had to lay the ghost of 1966 to rest. For once, let us enjoy our bit of glory – after all, our next slice might be a long time coming.

For an hour or so I listen to the moaners while the road-lights of Belgium pass me by, then sleep grabs hold and for me the day is over. For others, however, the night is only just beginning. The violence on the streets of Charleroi and Brussels continues long into the early hours. During the half-time interval it was reported that a mob of ticketless English fans trying to avoid being rounded up and held captive had rampaged down the main street of Charleroi, smashing windows and attacking locals as they went. This vandalism led to more than sixty fans' arrests, following which most of them were simply transferred on to the 12.30 a.m. train and sent packing without further charge. Throughout two days of violence in Charleroi, more than 450 English fans were detained and had their details registered by Belgian police. Many more were held but escaped with little more than a kick up the backside and a free lift back to the train station.

In Brussels, the violence grew more intense as the night wore on. The local Turkish and North African population hit the streets with a vengeance as they set about hunting down the reduced number of English supporters left in the Belgian capital, picking up from where they had left off the previous night. For once, local authorities appeared to be taking a more even-handed approach and detained many locals along with yet more English fans. Images of local Turkish lads lined up alongside their carefully prepared petrol bombs clearly demonstrated that much of the violence directed towards the English had been conceived in advance, while pictures of a lad strutting down the street brandishing a revolver indicated that there were also those among the local population more than willing to take the acrimony to even greater levels. Amazingly, these disturbing images were almost brushed aside by the English press and afforded only seconds on our news programmes, whereas the chair-throwing and aggressive singing involving English fans in the square up at Charleroi claimed hours of peak-time playback.

As midnight approached, the first wave of English fans returning from the Belgian mining town hit the streets of the capital. Numbers increased and so too did episodes of hooliganism. The Belgian authorities had instructed that no train carrying English fans should be allowed to stop in Brussels, but unfortunately their orders went unheeded: many did disembark at the Gare Du Midi station, and poured out into the local immigrant district. As the Turks threw their petrol bombs, the English steamed down the main drag, smashing windows and damaging cars. Behind them the two sets of fans left further evidence that those responsible for security arrangements had caused more problems than they had prevented. The sirens rang out loud well into the early hours of the morning as the number of English detained and deported in Brussels over the weekend edged its way towards 500. The weekend's violence had proved to be a heavy and yet perhaps predictable price to pay for the sake of a single international football match. And with so much money to be made from the game, go ahead it did, but unfortunately Belgium well and truly found itself picking up the tab.

PART FOUR
Romania

21

One Strike and You're Out!

Sunday 18 June 2000

England woke this morning from its drunken stupor a happier nation, shining in the afterglow of victory. Mainland Europe, meanwhile, rose to face the new day like a bear with a sore head. The weekend's feast of violence had left a sour taste in a lot of mouths, and now many people were beginning to ask some serious questions about the sickening things witnessed for its duration. For once, the British media find themselves stumped in terms of how to play the mood of the nation. Should they bask in the glory of victory or lead with the so-called 'scum' who've dragged the nation into the gutter? Elsewhere in Europe the situation is more clear-cut: England's team, its fans and the nation as a whole are once again labelled the scourge of Europe.

The images coming back at me through my television screen in no way reflect the scenes I witnessed with my own eyes. The money-shots relayed over and over: the chair-throwing and water cannons of Charleroi, the deported fans hiding their faces as they arrive back home, and the images of blood-stained English lads lined up in the streets while locals stood by clapping and cheering. All this mixed together provide a cocktail that the nation found hard to stomach. And yet I had been there, done it and seen none of it. Had I been fortunate? Had I, like so many others, mysteriously managed to exist on some parallel plane? While I was in Brussels and Charleroi I walked the very same streets and witnessed nothing more than two lads from the south coast trying to settle a domestic dispute. Back home, the media were telling me I'd just returned from a war-zone, a battlefield, a full-blown riot.

The part played in the violence by certain elements of the English following cannot be denied. The images clearly show that there were some wearing the red, white and blue who were only too happy to play out their game for the media circus. But studying the pictures, I can't help but wonder what's happened to all the footage involving the Turkish hooligans and the Germans and the heavy-handed retribution dished out by the Belgian police? Was this really a balanced view of what actually occurred on the streets of Belgium?

I found myself questioning once again the actions and the honesty of the Great British media. The hype surrounding the travelling English fans had been building for months as the public were whipped up into a frenzy of scared anticipation. The warnings grew more frequent as the tournament drew near. The networks had invested thousands in sending their news crews across the Channel, undercover reporters and their hidden cameras being the order of the day, in place of the usual sports units with their crisp, tailored suits. To the news crews, Eindhoven and Amsterdam undoubtedly proved a huge disappointment. By and large the English fans behaved, the Dutch police were happy and everything had gone just as they hadn't predicted. So when the circus moved south to Belgium they found themselves in desperate need of a result.

Many would argue that the scenes now filtering back through our television screens provided the media with their required result. Violent, blood-stained louts, scores of arrests and deported thugs returning home in huge numbers – everything they warned us about there for us all to see. But was the violence really on the scale they'd reported it to be? And were the English the only ones to blame for what we are now witnessing?

The scenes shot on the streets of Brussels were by far and

away the most dramatic, with huge mobs shown bursting out on to the streets from the bars and clubs lining the city's main highways. Pictures of lads pulling down advertising boards, fronting the police and chasing off the locals are all mixed together wonderfully with images of thugs getting their comeuppance, covered in blood, being beaten across the legs. Oh yes, this is just what the press were after. Forget Eindhoven and Amsterdam, here the English fans are displayed their true colours. Thugs, animals, scum, each and every one of them! Immediately after the event there was no inclination to provide a balanced argument – for now, it's all about shock with image after image flashing up before us. It's quick, punchy and in your face, snippets of information that fail to tell all that went before. Is it perhaps that a more balanced piece would leave the viewer confused, pose too many questions and cloud the issue even more than the tear gas did the crowds when it billowed from the bars and cafés? Or is it just easy, lazy journalism?

For now, the Turks with their knives, petrol bombs and guns are forgotten. Nobody's asking why the police used tear gas and empty bars indiscriminately. And they've failed to find out what the young lad did to warrant such a crack around the head with a truncheon, what charges are to be laid against him, if indeed any are. All that footage is for the time being brushed aside, no doubt only to be picked up, pieced together and edited into fifty-five dramatic minutes of television a few months down the line. The same reporters with them twisting and turning their words to give a counterview in the vain hope of restoring the equilibrium. But the damage has, of course, already been done.

The dramatic shots of water cannons sending people spinning across the square at Charleroi are played from every angle. Closer inspection of the incident, however, proves that most of those caught up in the chaos were mere bystanders and not the limited number of hooligans who set the ball rolling. The initial jets spurting out managed rather amusingly to disperse more camera crews than violent thugs anyway, as police set about targeting anything to get in their way. Surprisingly few news items appear to question the tactics adopted by the Belgian police. One thing the authorities tried out was the separation of the town into two halves by a line drawn down the middle over which opposing fans were not meant to cross. In theory this was a good plan but, incredibly, those in charge chose to sit back and watch as English and German mobs descended on the square, faced and taunted each other with nothing more than fresh air and a few yards of no-man's-land between them. They looked on for more than five hours, making their move only once the violence had gathered momentum. So much had been made of their zero-tolerance policy and their method of preventative arrests, and yet despite the previous night's warnings, despite the stabbing, the sporadic fighting and the bravado, they held back until that initial outburst had subsided. Shouldn't someone be asking why? Surely anyone with half a brain would have seen the potential for violence brewing. It wouldn't have needed a genius to work it out. Simply rounding up one of the mobs and removing them from the area would have prevented the confrontation. Just why this situation was allowed to fester we will never know. What's certain is that the introduction of the water cannon, coupled with the violent police baton-charge, had more people concerned for their safety than the initial small outbreak of hooliganism ever did.

What the media describe as a riot in truth amounted to nothing more than a hundred or so drunken English and German lads throwing plastic chairs and beer at each other. It looked ugly and it wasn't nice, but it was in no way a riot. The disturbance in the Place Charles II in Charleroi pales into insignificance when compared to the horrific events preceding it in Marseille, Istanbul and Copenhagen. In Charletoi there were no stabbings, no deaths and no serious injuries following the English and German fans clashes, just a few flying objects and people sent running for cover. Indeed, the majority of those sent bloodied and scurrying did so via the batons of the Belgian police who steamed in and hit out. As was the case with much of the footage from Brussels involving the Turks, the film showing the German hooligans' input at Charleroi mysteriously managed to work its way to the cutting-room floor as the media set about their agenda of blaming no one but the English for the violence and shame brought to Euro 2000.

The day wore on and the UEFA executive committee found themselves subject to intense media pressure as the world watched and waited with baited breath to see just how they were going to respond to the weekend's violence. In desperation, the Association's president, Lennart Johansson, called an emergency meeting and suddenly all eyes turned to focus on a small hotel room in the Belgian city of Liège. Fourteen of the fifteen committee members gathered together and the English FA, obviously expecting nothing more than a rap across the knuckles and a stiff ticking-off, sent security chief Sir Brian Hayes to face the music. To me, Sir Brian perfectly represents the lax approach it is commonly felt the English FA demonstrate towards combating the hooliganism associated with the national side. Just how this man has managed to hold on to his position as their chief security advisor following the shambles of France 98, I for one will never understand. I remember seeing Sir Brian address the world's press from the steps of a hotel in Toulouse, appearing both dazed and confused when challenged by reporters firing questions from all angles to which he offered no real answers. And yet here he was, two years down the line, up before the very same reporters and about to face those very same questions. Oh, how we've moved on!

For the committee there was only one item on the agenda: had time finally run out for English football and its violent following? The Swede Johansson must have felt the pain of what's happened more than most, because it was he who first instigated the move to have English domestic sides reinstated into European Cup competitions, thus putting an end to our five years in exile. He has long been a great fan of English football, but today, as the others closed ranks, his defensive stance was slowly but surely beaten back. Fighting in the opposite corner were the committee's chief executive, German national Gerhard Aigner, and the Turkish delegate, Senes Erzik.

Both men clearly having axes to grind as far as the English were concerned and with eager hands they snatched the opportunity to gain political Brownie points. For Mr Erzik, the English have become a long-term target. Following the stabbings in Istanbul he blamed the Leeds United fans while excusing his fellow countrymen. He took the same stance following the violence in Copenhagen and apparently employed the same tactic today in order to deflect criticism away from the violent Turkish fans seen fighting over the weekend. And so, with the back-up of those around him, he pressed for the ultimate penalty: the England team's immediate expulsion from the tournament.

If England were to be kicked into touch, so too would any chance the country had of staging the 2006 World Cup finals, and for the German delegate this provided a clear opportunity to edge his own country's alternative bid to host the world's greatest contest. For Mr Aigner, the job of swaying the doubters was made all the easier by the preventative measures taken by the German government prior to Euro 2000 kicking off. It didn't matter that the relatively small number of Germans present sparked much of the violence in Charleroi – for Aigner the point had already been prepared; Germany had at the very least made an effort towards dealing with their own hooligan problem, whereas the English, he argued, quite obviously had not. The debate went on well into the night, until eventually Sir Brian in his role as sacrificial lamb was given an ultimatum the FA never for one minute expected to hear: one more riot and you're out.

The news shattered the euphoria of victory and sent shockwaves back across the Channel and down through the corridors of England's training camp at Spa. Keegan, so long the champion of the English fans, appeared a broken man, his finest moment wrestled away from him and kicked into the shadows by political in-fighting and the handful of thugs scattered among the thousands who sung their hearts out in true support of his team. The Football Association's top bods suddenly found themselves with nowhere to hide and few answers to offer as they, along with the government, fell under increasing pressure to admit that they had done far too little too late to prevent England's violent football hooligans from reaching the streets of Belgium. But for the fans back home, and in particular those who travelled to Belgium in support of the team, the accusing finger was pointing in an entirely different direction. Kevin W. expresses a popularly held view:

> The British press should be hung, drawn and quartered for what they did to the thousands of genuine English fans out in Belgium. They treated us like dirt, branded us all the same. They're a disgrace, a bunch of parasites. And what they've done to English football is unforgivable. They've put the game in this country back ten years, all for the sake of some cheap-shot TV. Do they realise what they have done? Yes, there were a fair few idiots out in Belgium, we all know that. There always have and there always will be whenever England play abroad. You'll never get rid of them. But we're not all scum and I am sick of having to explain that to everyone I meet when I tell them I follow England. The people I work with, my parents and my wife and kids. My kids see that on the telly and must think I am never coming home! We all feel the shame the hooligans bring upon our country – they're scum. But there wasn't thousands of them like the media made it out to be, more like a few hundred. Just a few hundred out of 25,000 or so genuine fans that travelled out to support their country properly. But is that ever pointed out? Never!
>
> They're scum, the British press, scum. Everything has to be sensationalised, made out to be bigger than it is. They drag this country down. I am sure they get off on it all just as much. It's easy for them: find a few idiots, film them throwing the odd bottle and bingo, everybody's happy. The press have their money-shots and the idiots doing all the bottle-throwing think they'll return home to their mates some kind of national hero. But the press went too far this time, they were way out of line. The way they put over what happened in Charleroi was outrageous. I know, I was

there – and anyone else who was out there will tell you the same. You only have to look at that film. They made a mountain out of a molehill. You take a good hard look at what's going on the next time you see that film. That wasn't a riot, it wasn't even what most lads would put down as a decent row. But the press were so desperate to outdo each other they went into overdrive. If they'd have followed Millwall, Stoke or Cardiff last year they would have seen ten times worse than that! But no, they turned it into a riot and played right into the hands of UEFA, giving it to them on a plate. It's the same old easy get-out: pin it all on the English. Thanks to the British press the Belgian police – who, I have to say, behaved like animals – got off Scot free. They were the worst police I've seen by a mile. And the Turks got away with it on the grounds that they were provoked! Yeah, righto! What a load of old bull! I've got no sympathy for the press. I know a few of them got attacked out there, but when you see first hand how they change the story, I can't help thinking they sometimes get all they deserve.

The most ironic thing about it is that the British press have been covering up all the trouble that's been going on back home so as to help us get 2006 in the first place. They and the FA have been keeping things quiet for the last five or six years and yet here they blow the bid in two days! I bet Bobby Charlton and Geoff Hurst must be well pissed off. All that effort shot to pieces in two days! Notice how the German press played it? I mean, let's not forget they were involved as well. But what do they do? Keep their heads down, that's what. Keep their heads down and wait for the English press to dig themselves right in it. And look where it's got them; from nowhere they now have the World Cup finals. We won't see that being played here for at least another twenty years now! I didn't hear the Turkish press screaming out about their fans either.

But the British press have to go the other way and stoke up the hate. What is it with them? Why do they love to make all the English fans out to be such scum? It wasn't just the English playing up in Belgium, so why do they keep digging away at their own and never mention the rest of them and what else goes on? What about the thousands who steered clear of the trouble? There were 25,000 fans out in Charleroi – what about the rest of us who had a good time and mixed with the locals and the Germans no problem? What about all those who had just enjoyed the party and supported their country properly? There was nothing about them there, not a mention. English football has come on leaps and bounds over the last ten years. So why focus on a few idiots, idiots who shame, rather than the genuine fans who behave properly? Don't they realise that by focusing on the idiots they play right into their hands and make them out to be worth something.

When I first heard the news that they were threatening to throw us out I couldn't believe it. I thought, 'They have got to be joking, surely!' And then it sunk in that they were serious: one more riot and we're out. I tell you, if an English film crew were to have walked into our hotel that night they would have been slaughtered. By reporting the way they did, the press threatened to throw English football back to the Dark Ages. They made it so easy for the rest to pass the buck that we could have found ourselves out of the race and back in football isolation. It sickens me that they were prepared to do that to the game in this country. It sickens me that just in order to get some cheap TV they were prepared to risk the future of English football at a time when the game here is so on the up. I think the fans who really love this country and the team deserve an apology from the press in this country. They nearly cost us everything we had dreamed of.

Back home the media battled on regardless. Every chat show, radio phone-in and news item sucked the story dry as all the usual so-called 'experts', do-gooders and outspoken politicians were wheeled out and given their yearly fifteen minutes of fame. Most of those speaking so 'expertly' on the subject had never even set foot in Belgium. For Joe Public they said the right things, expressed a common outrage and demanded some answers. In parliament the home secretary, Jack Straw, soon found himself on the back foot as the opposition on all sides demanded to know just where his government had gone wrong in their efforts to prevent English hooligans from travelling abroad. In return Mr Straw had little to offer other than to point out that the vast majority of those fans deported from Belgium were not previously known to the British police in relation to football violence. Indeed, many of those who took an unexpected flight home had no criminal record whatsoever and included among their member barristers and civil engineers, the kind of people Jack Straw described as leading 'apparently law-abiding and respectable lives'. (Well, you wouldn't read about it, would you, eh?) Mr Straw went on to defend the government by adding: 'We can target those we know about, but it is much more difficult to target those who have never come to the attention of the police in the UK.' On closer inspection this statement offers plausibility to the claims made by many innocent fans concerning what really happened out in Brussels and Charleroi. Upon their arrival in the UK many of those people deported vehemently denied any involvement in the violence that had taken place. That, coupled with the fact that a lot of people also claimed to have been set upon by the Belgian police for doing nothing more than drinking in bars close to where the trouble occurred, perhaps suggests that some of these people might just be telling the truth. Surely Jack Straw's comments should have raised a few eyebrows at the very least, yet unfortunately everyone this side of the Channel appeared more interested in political point-scoring than in a quest for truth and justice.

Amazingly, apart from those deported fans claiming innocence, the only people displaying any concern about the tactics adopted by the Belgian police were the Belgians themselves. Through their local media, numerous bar-owners reported witnessing scenes of indiscriminate violence towards innocent fans and bystanders, confirming stories of the brutal use of both tear gas and batons on fans who had been doing nothing wrong. Others stated that while the English fans had been targeted, the local Turkish and African hooligans had been merely chased away from the mayhem in order that police could avoid making arrests of Belgian nationals. Indeed the zero-tolerance approach led to one section of the Belgian national press describing the police involved as 'out of control mavericks'. Unfortunately for their victims, back home the argument that there's no smoke without fire reigned supreme. All that is left for them is the long, hard struggle to clear their names, and the hope that sooner or later someone in government will sit up, take notice and listen to their side of the story.

There is no doubt that the heavy-handed police tactics employed during Euro 2000 provoked much condemnation among the English fans. One theory about what motivated such violence was believed by many but voiced by none: that the Belgian authorities had seized the opportunity for revenge for events that took place on their soil some fifteen years earlier. The Heysel disaster of 1985 scared European football to the bone, and in particular the three countries involved – England, Italy and Belgium. The Liverpool fans involved fully deserved their share of the blame for the horrific scenes witnessed live via television sets around the globe, but the Belgians also found themselves answerable to heavy criticism relating to their handling of the situation and to the safety of the now revamped stadium. The disaster is the most famous event in Belgian football history and yet had nothing to do with Belgian football, a fact which leaves a heavy cloud hanging over the nation. The fear that such a disaster might repeat itself must have weighed heavy on the Belgian authorities in the build-up to the 2000 tournament, especially when placed against the concerns raised over the safety of the stadium at Charleroi. And many believed that this fear led to the implementation of the extreme aggression vented upon the English fans.

The violence directed towards the English clearly far

outweighed that dished out to fans of other nationalities and, when looked at in the cold light of day, the 'payback' theory is one I find hard to argue against. What fuels such speculation for me are the images of blood-stained English fans lined up in the streets, handcuffed and ridiculed by locals – compared with pictures of local youths being led away to police vans with nothing more than a helping hand to guide them. To me, it seems that once again the English were being made to pay for the legacy of days gone by, a debt to be cleared with the spilling of English blood.

For some, however, the violence witnessed in Belgium is not what it seems to others. I met Steve on a train travelling up to Liverpool some weeks after Euro 2000 had finished. He supports Man City and, like a lot of lads, was involved in violence back in the 70s. Although his view differs from my own, I feel it's only right that he has his say:

I don't think much of what you saw with England in Charleroi and Brussels was really football violence. Not what I'd call football violence, anyway. I think we just live in a violent society now and that lads will look for anything to tag on to in order to get that aggression out of their system. Real football violence was about taking another team's home end, taking their pub and sorting out a meeting place where you could have it away. You don't get that with England, but that was really what being a football hooligan was all about: taking someone's end. It's not throwing plastic chairs at lines of riot police or mouthing off for the cameras. When I was at it we used to do all we could to avoid the police; these lads head straight for the main square as if they're looking for them. I think any of those lads would be doing exactly the same on any Saturday night in their towns back home – they're just pissed-up lads looking for trouble. Most of them never had tickets and loads didn't even travel further than Brussels. I think most of them are out there because they're proud to be English, but much of the time it's just an excuse for a piss-up and the chance to play up. Even the arrest figures said most of them had no previous football convictions! I think the problem still exists back here, but if the Germany game would have been played on a Tuesday night I don't think half as many lads would have travelled out – they'd have been back home getting pissed and fronting up to our own police instead.

While England slipped into mourning, the tournament moved on. Spain beat Slovenia 2–1 and Yugoslavia won 1–0 against Norway, a side more dull than a wet weekend in Grimsby. But when set against the rest of the day's events none of that actually seemed to matter.

22

All for One and One for All . . .
Unless, Of Course, You're English!

Monday 19 June 2000

If ever proof were needed that English football has to exist by a totally different set of rules to those found in the rest of the world, then today was to provide that proof. Less than twenty-four hours after the England team were threatened with expulsion from the tournament as a consequence of the actions of their violent fans, the streets of Belgium played host to yet more disturbances. Only this time the actions of the hooligans involved drew a quite different response from those who had been so outspoken the previous evening.

Following their 2–0 victory over the host nation, victorious Turkish fans took to the streets of Brussels and went on the rampage. At one stage a mob of an estimated 1500 Turks and North African immigrants converged on the Bourse in the centre of the city, from where they set about attacking passing vehicles and seeking out the bars containing both English and Belgian supporters. During the ensuing violence the hooligans wrecked two bars and sent people running for cover at every turn. The mob hurled bricks, bottles and paving slabs through the windows of the Au Pot Carré bar, where a dozen or so English fans were found sitting with fans from Sweden, Italy, Norway and Belgium. The Belgian owner of the bar, Thierry de Groot, described the attack as vicious and unprovoked and said that 'the English were drinking quietly and then the Turks stormed the bar'. He said that he felt the police stood back and did nothing because of the fact that it was the English who were victims of the attack. Further down the Rue de la Fourche the rampaging mob continued their trail of destruction, throwing an array of missiles at English fans drinking outside the Lop Lop bar. Their antics went unchallenged by the police for several minutes and forced the English fans inside the bar, until eventually 100 officers in riot gear put in an appearance and dispersed the baying mob.

The mayhem left glass littering the streets, people fearful for their lives and two businessmen with their source of income in tatters. And yet in a quite unbelievable instance of double standards, the accusing finger was pointed not towards the Turks but in the direction of the English. In order to cover their own backs, both UEFA and the mayor of Brussels performed an incredible U-turn. UEFA's chief executive, Gerhard Aigner, so vocal in calling for the English to be banned the previous night, quite sickeningly dismissed the Turkish riot as nothing more than 'a joyful party that went wrong', and refused to condemn the hooligans or level any sanctions towards those involved. Astonishingly, Brussels' mayor, Francois-Xavier de Donnea, went even further, actually explaining away the actions of those hell-bent on violence by claiming they had previously been 'psychologically attacked' by the English and were merely seeking out revenge for the events of the previous few days.

These statements and allegations should have had the English FA along with many of our politicians banging the table in utter disgust, but UEFA were allowed to turn their backs and carry on regardless. Such an outbreak of violence might at the very least have motivated UEFA to call another emergency meeting, bring the Turkish fans to book and dish out the same threat to their national team as was given to the English the previous night. But no, quite unashamedly UEFA, and our own right-on politicians, did nothing, refusing to make even the slightest attempt to disguise the double standards they so happily apply when dealing with English football and its followers. Just how and why those involved got away with such outrageous slurs on the innocent English fans trapped inside those bars I'll never know. As was the case in Italy 1990 and France 98, English football fans were finding out that defending their rights is an unpopular option for the powers that be.

Following the violence in Charleroi and Brussels, the former sports minister Tony Banks referred to the English fans as 'xenophobic' – a term often levelled at English football fans on foreign soil. But is it any wonder that many turn in on themselves when they are so openly treated like lepers and outcasts whenever they venture out on to mainland Europe? Europe stands shoulder to shoulder while clearly displaying a dislike and distrust for all that is English – exactly the same xenophobic dislike we find ourselves labelled with, and a distrust that works both ways, as the stance taken by UEFA demonstrates.

It sickens me to think that those concerned can be so open about their hate for all that is English and simply carry on regardless. It sickens me to think that our football will never be allowed to free itself from the past, while others freely commit the same acts of violence unchecked and unchallenged. And it sickens me that no one from our government, from our press or from within our football itself has got the balls to get up and make a stand against these people who love to sweep our national sport and this country down into the gutter. For until someone takes up that challenge, it is in the gutter that English football and its army of fans will stay.

In the day's other match Italy manage to keep their 100 per cent record by defeating the Swedes in Eindhoven, a result that means the boys in their nice tight kit now head off to Brussels for a quarter-final against either England or Turkey – to be played in the stadium previously known as Heysel! Once again, everyone is holding their breath.

23

Over and Out

Tuesday 20 June 2000

It's 8.05 a.m. and as I travel down the escalator towards the EuroStar booking office at Waterloo station, I'm continually asking myself why I'm even bothering to make this trip. Over the past two days UEFA's backbiting and double-crossing has rammed home to me everything I now despise about this once great game and those who profess to control it. I have also left setting out on this trip until late because I didn't want to hang around in a town that could well turn into a battle-ground, so I can't help but think of just turning around, saving my money and going down the pub to watch the game like everyone else.

At times like this I can be a right miserable bastard. But suddenly life pops up and gives me a little pat on the head as if to say, 'Ed, don't be such a tit. You know you want to go really!' – and it seems that God's once again decided to help me out. This time he's sent an angel bearing gifts, in the guise of a small geek of a bloke wearing a shellsuit and glasses. He approaches from nowhere and asks whether or not I need a ticket for tonight's match. He asks for a ton and once I stop laughing I offer him all the cash I have on me: £45. He accepts and praise the Lord, off we go again! Is life always going to be this simple, or am I just a lucky bastard? I quickly work out that I have had to shell out just £120 on tickets in order to see all of England's opening matches – what a result! Suddenly a smug little thought enters my mind: 'Ah-ha, David Davies, I piss on your Travel Club, your membership fees and your lotteries for tickets – for with my ticket, I win!'

Having picked myself up from the floor after hearing EuroStar's request for £145 to book a one-way ticket to Brussels (!), I tell them to go forth and multiply before heading off to Waterloo East, from where I bunk the 9.03 a.m. down to Dover. My luck runs out at this point as the ticket inspector catches me at Folkestone and demands I buy a ticket. Cheeky bastard! As I make my way through passport control to catch the 12.15 sailing to Calais, I am stopped by the immigration officer, who recognises my name and starts to ask a few questions. Following all the political spoutings of the last few days, I'm worried he might refuse me entry, but he eventually lets me through. I then go about the business of trying to find someone travelling from Calais down to Charleroi by car and with a spare seat on offer. On the ferry with me are three coachloads of England fans, all of whom are on a freebie thanks to winning some computer game competition on a local radio station last night! After a quick chat with one of the lucky winners I find out that not all the coaches are full, so I hunt down the main man to see if I can cadge a lift. He takes one look at me, sees the shaved head, tells me all seats are taken and then turns his back! Yeah well, cheers. That'll be the last time I poke any of Lara Croft's buttons!

The lucky winners appear to be the only English fans on board besides me and three Everton fans heading off to work in Paris, so once the ferry docks I make a mad dash for the bus to the train station and can't resist the opportunity to give the freeloaders the old finger as I go. On arriving at the station I find that my timing is tighter than a gnat's chuff, as the only connection for Charleroi has me travelling via the French town of Lille, from where I'll move over the border into Belgium and arrive at my final destination less than fifty minutes before kick-off! The journey down to Lille is hot, slow and lonely, and once again I wonder why I am here. Is it to do with the football, or is it because of something else entirely? What is it that has me, like so many others, travelling mile upon mile, spending pound after pound? As the French countryside passes me by I come to the conclusion that for me, this particular journey is being made for rather different reasons than usual following all the recent condemnation of everything English. Don't get me wrong, I love the football. I love the beauty of the game, the skill and the gracefulness of it all. But what takes place out there on the lush green turf forms only a small part of this trip, which has become more of a mission fuelled by my resentment of all those who have stood against England and the English over the past few days.

Unlike many of the politicians and do-gooders spouting off back home, I've never been ashamed to be English. Of course, there are many things I dislike about our country – the class system, old people dying of the cold in their own homes, the nurses getting paid less than parliamentary pen-pushers, and the fact that people still find themselves sleeping on the streets while others eat off golden cutlery – to name but a few. But the more people tell us we are scum, the more determined I become to prove them wrong, especially when those people so blatantly deny their own shortcomings. The more they try to knock us down, the stronger grows my desire to stand up to them, for there may well be much wrong on England's shores but it is far outweighed by all that is right. I am sick of hearing all Englishmen being described as xenophobic by the rest of Europe when we display any form of national pride. This is, after all, national pride for a country built upon the cornerstone of allowing people to enter it, escape persecution and free themselves from a life of hell. What sickens me more, however, is the fact that most of those pointing an accusing finger in our direction are only too keen to hurry lorryload after lorryload of asylum seekers through their own borders in order to get them to England and out of their own backyard as quickly as possible! Being English is something to be proud of and it is for this reason I am making this journey.

*　*　*

As the train pulls into Lille Flandres station I realise that I am no longer an Englishman alone, for sitting in the next compartment along from mine are Dean and Darrias who, like me, have been chasing the clock in order to make kick-off. To my surprise Dean is blessed with both living in Hertfordshire and following the Hornets, while Darrias has the double misfortune of living south of the River Thames and supporting Man U! Just hearing an English accent restores my faith in life, though, and so with an hour and a half to kill we head out of the station and enter the nearest bar. I soon learn that this is to be their first ever trip abroad in support of the national side, and whereas Dean seems certain of victory, Darrias believes the Romanians to be no pushover – adding weight to his argument by pointing out our weakness in defence compared to their power up front.

As the pair of them have never witnessed England away first hand, I ask them what they made of all the publicity back home concerning the violence. Not surprisingly they'd thought twice about making the trip. Indeed, if it wasn't for the fact that they bought their tickets a good few weeks ago, they would have definitely stayed back home and made their usual trip down the pub instead. As it is, neither of them is wearing England colours and they too have made the decision to stay out of Charleroi until the last possible minute, just in case.

At 7.58 p.m. the train pulls into Charleroi and the three of us step on to the platform. Immediately it strikes me that this is a totally different Charleroi to the one I experienced just three days ago. Nowhere to be seen are the English en masse, singing their hearts out and announcing their arrival. Gone are the hordes of police with their dogs and riot gear, and the concrete plaza that fronts the station is quiet. My first task is to ask a policeman if any local Turks are scouring the streets around the station in the hope of picking up the odd lost English fan. He looks puzzled before going on to tell me that there has been no trouble on the streets of Charleroi today. As we make our way up towards the stadium, the streets have an uneasy calm, as if the party has already happened and we have arrived just in time to help clean the place up. The stories I told the lads about walking into a town overrun by English must seem far-fetched, as the few hundred disappointed fans without tickets either trudge their way to the half-empty bars or support their drunken friends as they stumble through the litter. Gone are the mounted police-horses, no riot cops and no helicopter flying overhead. Missing is the excited atmosphere of a major international football match.

Once up at the ground, we make our way through the tree-lined walkways that backs on to the three-tiered stand housing those of us with the Green Sector marked on our black-market tickets. I save the lad on the gate the trouble and check the ticket myself: Entrance 3, Block R2, Row 26, Seat 178. Oh, and the name upon the ticket: UEFA! The three of us go our separate ways and within minutes I find myself sitting among the type of people I would much rather avoid, and who I think share the same feelings upon first seeing yours truly. Shit! It's the shirt, jacket and tie brigade.

They sit, chat and clap politely while I want to rant, sing and abuse. Dotted around I notice more of my own, all looking for support but hopelessly outnumbered by the corporate free-loaders, their wives and work associates. To my right the English fans sing and dance, and down to my left the Romanians make more noise than their meagre numbers merit as they battle to out-sing the few hundred English fans tucked in the right-hand corner of their end. A drunk lad comes walking up the gangway towards me. He stops, turns and starts singing at the top of his voice. From the back someone shouts for him to sit down, a request to which he spits the following retort: 'Fuck off, you cunt!'

Most people around us fall silent, while a few others and I crack up laughing. Them and Us mixing happily! There was a time when walking through the turnstiles was seen as a great leveller; now it would seem football has created a greater divide.

The game starts, the mood is subdued and then Romania score. It's a lucky goal, a fluke by some spawny git and I am desperate to tell him so, but I remain rooted as those around me talk it through and discuss Nigel Martyn's positioning. Once again England find themselves outplayed, outclassed and out of their depth. Gary Neville misses yet another tackle: 'Neville, you useless fuck!'

This time I have left my seat, only to find myself standing alone with nothing more than a frightened over-the-shoulder glance from the unfortunate husband and wife team occupying the seats directly in front of me. She looks shocked and he looks disgusted. I slowly slip back down into my seat and hear myself say the word I never thought I would say: 'Sorry.'

It tears at my stomach. What has come over me? What am I saying *sorry* for? For a moment I had given in – given in to them and their sterile way of watching football. A voice in my head tells me it's all over, that football will never be the same for me again and that it's time to divorce myself from my love. The time has come to get up and go, take up tiddlywinks and masturbation rather than give in and become one of them. Then something clicked. I jumped from my seat and yelled at the top of my voice for no apparent reason: 'NEVILLE, YOU CUNT!'

Fuck giving in! This is my arena as much as theirs – and it always will be!

Against the run of play, England score. As the rest of the stadium erupts, those in block R2 clap and shake hands – a more surreal display of restrained emotion it would be hard to imagine. I feel like a leper at a kissing-contest as I congratulate myself and then gesture to the other lost and lonely souls dotted around the section. For five minutes England start to play; the referee gives a penalty and at half-time we go in 2–1 ahead. The time has come for me to escape.

Walking beneath the concrete stand I bump into Pete from Northampton and feel a sense of normality wash over me. He talks football on my terms, slags the players and the tactics and praises our luck. Welcome back to the real world! Joining him for the second half I find myself sitting bang on the halfway-line and right in among the radio-competition winners I met travelling out on the ferry. I spot the bloke who refused to give me a lift and give him the same finger gesture I offered up at

Calais, for if that's what he expected then why not give it to him?

The second half kicks off and the England fans give their all, but the players are unable to respond. Nigel Martyn punches when he should have caught and the ball is fired back into the open empty net: 2–2. The clock ticks away, time ebbing slower, slower. Pete and I stare blankly, both of us subdued, all the time knowing, just *knowing* that, because it's England, sooner or later it's all going to go terribly wrong.

The ball is knocked wide for the Romanian winger. Without hesitation he pushes it into the box and ghosts past Neville. The English lad chases, lunges, fouls. Penalty! The Romanian fans go caveman while the English shake their heads in knowing expectation. A minute later the ball hits the back of the net. Like many of those around me I stand arms crossed and say nothing. As I stare into space I think of Scotland. I think of the Turks, the Germans, the rest of the world. At this moment they'll all be going mental, celebrating England's demise and bathing in the glory of our downfall. The whistle blows and once again England have failed.

I shake Pete's hand then leave him standing. I've seen this sight so many times I don't need yet another reminder. Outside, the mood is one of pre-ordained expectance rather than anger. In our hearts I think we all knew, we all knew we were never good enough. In fact, we weren't even at the races. I run the question over and over as I walk the back-streets to the station. How can a side play that poorly? There was no way we could blame it on bad luck. We had all the luck going our way tonight. No, we were just shite, left floundering. Pure fucking pants!

Once at the station, I find the usual disorganisation you come to expect. There are no trains to Brussels, just buses, and the riot police block the station entrance, refusing to let anybody in or know what the hell is going on. As the numbers grow so too does the tension. Three coppers tell me there is no train to Calais, but when other fans back my claim that there is, the shields come up and the pushing starts. Eventually a guard appears to confirm that the 12.30 a.m. train is indeed Calais-bound, and one by one the anxious police allow us to squeeze through and on to the platform. The station is heaving but the mood is tired and limp. I spot Dean and Darrias, the pair of them looking like fully paid-up members of the Pissed-Off and Disappointed Club. I can't help thinking that for them the England away experience has probably now been done and dusted.

The first train is due to leave at 11.30 pm and is heading for Ostende and, as the general feeling among the fans is to just get back home as soon as possible, the majority climb aboard and fight for the seats. Once the train pulls out, a calm descends and the police relax their stance. All the refreshment machines have been switched off so I head out of the station in search of lard and bump into Kevin Miles, frontman for the Football Supporters' Association. For Kevin the last few days have proved to be just a little bit taxing. He looks tired and drawn, not surprising for a man who has found himself at the twenty-four-hour beck and call of the world's press. In the past I've not been a great fan of the FSA, but on this occasion I have to shake the man's hand for being brave enough to not cave in when the going got tough as he tells me that so far, to the best of his knowledge, only three fans out of all the hundreds deported have ended up getting charged with any kind of offence.

It's a statistic that tells its own story, and yet Kevin could repeat it to the press over and over and they wouldn't hear a word of it. His organisation is fighting a battle it has little chance of ever winning. No one cares in the short-term about what they so readily see as the English scum. It's so easy to spit hate from the pages of a paper. So simple to pen righteous words that condemn and disassociate. Digging beneath the surface to give balance to a story takes effort and a certain degree of morals, something the vast majority of England followers believe the media gave up on years ago. But above all it takes time – and in their desperate rush to meet deadlines and live links, time is never on the media man's side, so the shock-mentality takes over and the easy option kicks in. Kevin could stand before the prying cameras, relaying the fact that he was there and had witnessed much of the action himself, and would still be branded a liar by those sitting in a studio some 400 miles away – purely because the angle they want on the story will never fit in with the grim reality of the truth. That's England away as seen by the British media for you. Unfortunately it has been since the 70s, and it will probably always remain so in their rush to be first with the headline.

Our train back to Calais is virtually empty, twelve carriages long with less than a hundred pissed-off fans on board and not one ticket purchased between them. As we cross the border into France, the train draws to a halt and we stare out the windows at the French riot police waiting to do us over if we dare step out of line. Looking at their guns and their wide, aggressive stance, we comment on the fact that if they weren't so laughable they'd be quite frightening. On arriving at the northern French port there is more of the same to greet us. This time we are held in a pen like prisoners of war, and so at 4.00 a.m. a low-whistled version of the *Great Escape* theme breaks out, sending a smile across my face and a shiver down my back as for a moment I imagine seeing this same scene some sixty years back. The image is suddenly shattered because not everyone likes our tune: the dogs are woken with a bang on the van so they can drown out our chorus with their vicious barking – just a little reminder for us not to take the piss too much. But I don't mind, the piss has already been taken!

While on the ferry I'd managed to cadge a lift back to Harrow, where I buy a paper telling me that England were shit. Well fuck me, at last the press have got something right! However, what English football needed to do now was pick through the bones and try to work out why it had all gone so horribly wrong.

PART FIVE
Aftermath

24

Smells Like Team Spirit

I hope you don't mind, but at this point I'd like to try something out on you. It's a new game I've been working on, a kind of Fantasy Football-meets-Cluedo thing that I feel might just catch on in the boardrooms up and down the country. So, pen and paper at the ready and here we go.

Pick any one of the following players:

> Stan Collymore
> Nicolas Anelka
> Emmanuel Petit
> Paolo Di Canio
> Pierre van Hooijdonk
> Ugo Ehiogu

Now pick one of the following managers;

> Brian Clough
> Bill Shankly
> John Gregory

Now pick one of the following implements:

A gun
A hammer
A red-hot poker
A well-polished size-nine steel-toe-capped boot

And finally, pick one of the following locations:

The manager's office
The training ground
The local home-supporters' pub on match day
The arse

You should end up with some kind of Collymore-Gregory-poker-arse package, something I am sure would delight almost every football fan in the country and in particular those who follow Aston Villa FC. Well, what do you reckon? Personally I like it. I like it because it reflects the feelings I have towards much of what is happening in the modern game as the balance of power shifts and players – especially those with egos bigger than the Third World debt – take control. I remember the days when the managing of a team was left, as you would expect, to the manager. I remember the days when if the boss said you were dropped, then you were dropped. Or, more importantly, the days when if the boss said you were playing, then at £30,000 a week you bloody well played. Days I fear we are likely never to see again.

The influence player-power currently holds over football is immense, a modern-day disease that not only undermines the abilities of many club managers but also displays a distinct lack of respect for the game's paying customers. Many greeted the relegation from the top flight in May 2000 of those Premier League perennial fighters Wimbledon FC with a sigh of relief. Surely within their demise, however, there was a lesson for us all, as a single season of egotistical in-fighting coupled with dressing-room bust-ups put their loyal following through hell and simultaneously sent the club crashing out of the top flight. Throughout the season, the club's star players voiced their disapproval of newly appointed manager, Egil Olsen, undermining his authority and spreading unrest throughout the club in a disgraceful and disrespectful display of near mutiny. Surely the time for airing such views was once the spectre of relegation had been laid to rest and the close season had fallen, rather than when the battle was still raging. But when the club sank into the trenches it found its more influential players not standing shoulder to shoulder, as one would expect, but posting transfer requests and challenging the opposition in the players' tunnel rather than out on the playing field, where their presence was really needed.

It is not only smaller clubs such as Wimbledon that are falling victim to this new disease, as the followers of Aston Villa FC have found to their cost on more than one occasion. An outspoken chairman coupled with an even more outspoken manager make for a hard pill to swallow, something the more sensitive souls to pass through Villa Park realised when faced with a few home truths. However, when a club of Villa's stature starts having players posting transfer requests on the grounds that they want to pull on the shirt of a 'bigger' club, I believe the time has come for us all to sit up and take note. For if it can happen at Villa, it can happen anywhere. I met Aston Villa fan Greenie on the way home from Charleroi and he told me exactly how he felt about the way certain players from his club had behaved in the build-up to Euro 2000:

It's unbelievable. They have the greatest job in the world: professional footballer – the dream job – money the rest of us could only ever dream of. They're treated like film stars wherever they go and the fans love them. What more could they want? It's just greed, pure greed. The way they have treated the Villa faithful is an absolute disgrace. I've got no respect for Southgate any more and I never want to see him in a Villa shirt again. He's not fit to wear it. He wants to move to a 'bigger' club, does he! Is the man a fucking idiot? A bigger club! For fuck's sake, we're Aston Villa – one of the top six clubs in the country! What kind of reaction does he honestly expect to get the next time he runs out at Villa Park? He'll get slaughtered by the fans, slaughtered. As a Villa fan I came out here to support Southgate, just like loads of the other Villa lads I've met, but fuck him now, I couldn't give a shit about the man. If I were John Gregory I'd send the bastard off to train with the kids until he can get shot of him, see how he likes that! He might be an England international but if he doesn't want to play for the club he's no good to us, so send him off with the kids. Thing is, you can't do that any more – no one will buy a player who's out of the first team so Gregory's got to play him, ain't he?

The trouble we've had with players at Villa, fucking hell! Collymore, Dwight Yorke, Carbone, Ehiogu. Ehiogu, what a joke. He wants to leave Villa because he thinks the club holds him back from playing for England! It didn't stop Keegan picking Southgate and Gareth Barry, did it? What a prick! The egos of these players now are so big. They're basically saying they think they are bigger than any club. They think they are better than the Villa deserve and then they get upset when we get on their backs! What they're really saying is that the club I love isn't good enough for them. Right, if that's the case, then fuck off. Let's see how well you do elsewhere.

I'll be Villa until I die – I love the club and I don't want people pulling on the shirt who feel any different. You see, Gregory tells it like it is and they can't handle it. I love the man. I'd rather have him there, kicking the arses, than some 'yes' man. He gets a bit of stick about the way we play but his record speaks for itself. I only want to see players at Villa who want to be there, and Gregory's the same so he'll do for me. Deadly Doug's done well to stick with him when many thought he'd kick him out before now. God only knows what we'd have won had we had a full team of players who had a bit of balls about them and played for the manager. I'd love to see Gregory get the England job one day. He's perfect for it – just like

Clough was – but he won't get it because he's not a 'yes' man. He wouldn't put up with shit from anyone and that'd soon sort out the men from the boys, and then maybe we'd at least have a team who look like they're trying.

The problem that dogs managers such as John Gregory is, of course, money as chairmen leap upon the transfer merry-go-round and buy into outrageous contract demands, pushing the stakes ever higher. Inflated by vast transfer fees, the players have become ever greater commodities rather than loyal servants to the club.

This has led us into a situation where if the price is right any player is available, no matter who he is! In a time when football is awash with money and when the demands for success are immediate the players, under the guidance of their agents, are realising their worth and constantly pulling at the pursestrings. Suddenly a new five-year contract might as well be a five-minutes one as player-loyalty goes out the window and player-commodity takes over. The demands now being placed within our footballers' contracts are borderering on the ridiculous. Surely no one can deny that wages have spiralled out of control – £30,000-plus per week is nothing short of madness. Wages like this will one day send many clubs crashing out of existence, but the required addition to the contracts of the promise of a new car, a house and numerous free trips home to go *with* such a wage is doing nothing but taking the piss. Many players have worked themselves into such a strong financial position that they now hold their clubs over a barrel, as their worth demands a place within the squad-shop window no matter how strongly the manager protests or how poor their current form. However, there is one clause now common within contracts that riles me more than any other, that being the get-out-of-jail clause many players now insist on having installed, and which can be used should the club they are signing for find themselves suddenly relegated come the end of the season.

This clause is insulting beyond belief. As a fan all I can ask for is that the players give 100 per cent whenever they go on to the field. I expect them to display the same commitment to the cause as I do, to play with pride and passion and to carry with them the responsibility their signing has placed upon their shoulders. Such a get-out clause frees them of all such responsibility. It allows them to walk away should the worst happen and relieves them of the duty I feel they should have to try and put things right. And so, how are we to stop such an epidemic from spreading and also just who are the right people to administer the cure if the current situation continues?

With the Football Association's hands tied by European law regarding a maximum wage cap, the solution can only come from our clubs' chairmen, those who to a certain extent initiated the problem in the first place. The initial weakness many displayed by caving in to the outrageous transfer demands placed by agents has led to a situation only they can correct. No matter how sickening the greed demonstrated by certain players appears, the realities of living in a world where money means everything makes it hard to point an accusing finger in their direction – after all, the offer of more money for doing the same job is something most of us would find hard to refuse. The only true way out is for the club chairmen to get tough. Unfortunately, though, with yet another huge influx of money coming into the game via the signing of new television deals, those days seem to have been put back even further. When the Football Association announced details of the new multi-million-pound television package, they trumpeted the negotiations as a triumph for the fans, when in reality the only ones dancing to the tune of the cash registers were the players and their agents. Until the day arrives when chairmen, managers and fans who feel £30,000 a week in wages is a piss take stand up as one and say enough is enough, the players' grip on the game will strengthen even further, handing them a stranglehold strong enough to bring any club to its knees – something I am sure the fans of Wimbledon FC will be only to pleased to tell you.

* * *

However, through the clouds there could well be a silver lining on the horizon. Many believe that the European Union's proposed move to scrap football's current transfer system could turn the game on its head overnight and send many clubs into oblivion. But is that really so, or are we about to see the introduction of some much-needed sanity into a sport that has gone totally money mad? Under the new proposals, transfer fees for players could become a thing of the past as footballers suddenly find themselves granted the same working rights as all other employees, thus enabling them to terminate their contracts and move clubs at just a few weeks' notice. However, coupled with such legislation are also rights for the employers, rights which if viewed wisely could well see our clubs beginning to wrestle back some of the power that has slipped through their fingers. Suddenly those players with egos the size of the Amsterdam Arena and with mouths to match could find their disruptive influence buying them a one-way ticket to the dole queue – something sure to restrain even the most arrogant voices within the dressing-room. With no vast transfer fee hanging over their heads, unruly players may well be left out in the cold and training with the kids as our managers regain control and begin to flex some muscle of their own. All of a sudden the issue of job-security would become paramount when players, their agents and the chairmen sit down to discuss new terms. Perhaps this is a twist in the current thinking that could well afford our chairmen the luxury of introducing a few extra safety clauses of their own, such as loyalty payments, long-service bonuses and performance-related pay structures!

Of course, the main concern within all this is that a major source of income for our smaller clubs will disappear, something many fear will herald the end for some and send others crashing to their knees. But again I wonder whether or not this is the truly the case. Could it be that football is at last having to wake up to the cold realities of the modern game? I remember many within the game expressing the same fears following the introduction of the Bosman Ruling, and yet this saw the game prosper like never before with more players becoming millionaires, clubs' share-prices rocketing and crowds increasing. However, the days when Manchester United, Liverpool and Arsenal continue to play in a professional domestic set-up alongside the likes of Carlisle, Port Vale and Watford are coming to an end. For far too long many of our smaller clubs have been living above their means, and while the gap between the rich and poor grows ever wider we all have to accept that football as we see it now just can't continue – the European Super-League, when it comes, will inevitably pick the cream of the crop and take the money from the bottom. Again I see the situation not as all doom and gloom, but rather as a possible new beginning because clubs will be forced into nurturing new home-grown talent instead of giving inflated handouts to those born further afield. Unlike many, I believe that the proposed system will see an upturn in youth development as wage bills become tighter and expensive foreign paycheques a thing of the past. Many clubs will be forced into relying on their youth policy in order to balance their books, and that should in turn open the door for our young stars of the future. A future English football most certainly needs nurturing!

There is no doubt that English football is balancing on the brink of major change, but if it is to ever regain some of its stature then major change is just what is required. However, as the game braces itself for yet another shake-up, one thing is certain. Looking on, taking it all in and waiting with baited breath will be those who remain most loyal: the fans. And while some would say, 'Cheer up, it might never happen!' I personally prefer the option, 'Cheer up, it's just about to!'

25

Not-so Poor Old Johnny Foreigner

The notion that the influx of foreign players on to our shores has been good for English football is, quite frankly, bollocks. Good for the English Premier League, yes, but for English football? I don't think so. I don't for one minute doubt the talent many foreign players have brought to our domestic competition but, as the England team's display at Euro 2000 clearly demonstrated, the price we've paid in order to have such an exciting league has been a very high one indeed.

The declaration made by Kevin Keegan prior to the tournament stating that he believed future England managers would be having to scout much of their international talent from the Nationwide Leagues proves beyond doubt that English football is now nothing more than second rate – a stark truth we all have to face up to if we are ever to reach the heights we constantly kid ourselves to be our God-given right. The instigation of our Premier League was originally the Football Association's blueprint for putting English football back on the map. Yet rather than become the breeding-ground for our own flesh and blood, it has become nothing more than a stomping-ground for Europe's cash-hungry stars in search of the best deal their agents can find. The 'must win now' mentality currently running the game instead of the need to build for the future has led to our clubs searching the globe for a quick fix in preference to nurturing the country's youth, and with time being the one thing clubs fail to hold control over, it is hard to see how we can ever reverse that trend.

For the Football Association there is no immediate answer. As the Frankenstein's monster they have created wrestles free from their grasp, so agents along with their lawyers stifle every move they make towards introducing a limit on foreign players or the implementing of a maximum wage cap. When Chelsea FC became the first domestic side to field a team containing not one English player, the FA surely had to hold up their hands and admit that their master-plan had backfired in a way no one had ever thought possible. To me, the Blues are no longer seen as an English club, rather as a European club just waiting for the great escape to the Promised Land. I find it hard to imagine how many of the older Chelsea fans can stand back and watch that happen to their club when the likes of Osgood, Harris and Wilkins still live strong in the memory. The claims made by influential people such as the Chelsea chairman Ken Bates that the foreign imports have helped improve the quality of our own stars is again, I believe, nothing but a carefully worded smoke-screen designed to cloud his desire to build London's representatives for the coming of the European Super-League. (A Super-League in which London is likely to find itself represented by a mix of Italians, Frenchmen, Africans, South Americans and Scandinavians!) However, as is always the case, not everyone shares my view, so I allow my good mate and Chelsea season-ticket holder David to have his say:

Basically I couldn't give a toss where they come from. Black, white, yellow or brown, I couldn't give a monkey's. As long as they're doing the business I don't care; that's all that counts. It's no good going on about the old days, you've got to face up it: football's changed. It's a totally different game now to what it was five or six years ago. It's a world game, you have to be in there with the big guns, and if that means having some geezer from Italy rather than Islington banging them in the back of the net then do I care? No, I don't think I do! Ken Bates has got to make sure we are the best team in London because when the European Super-League comes around there's only going to be room for one London club. So we've *got* to be the best. It don't matter how much it costs or from what part of the planet we get the players, we have to get ahead – and stay ahead – of Arsenal. We have to!

You can go on about the England side until you're blue in the face, but international football ain't really nothing but a sideshow now. I love England and I'd love to see us stuffing every other bastard, but you only have a meaningful tournament every two years. As a fan I want to win now, not hang on to the slim hope England might do something every two years. That's no good to me, is it? What am I meant to do, sit around and watch a pile of crap in the meantime? Sorry, but I had enough of that in the past, thanks very much. Of course, I would love to see more English players coming through, but we just haven't got them: simple. If Arsenal or United are going out and buying abroad we can't sit back – Bates would never get away with that, not with the amount of money we have to pay. Actually, unlike most, I ain't that bothered about the cost at Chelsea. It's a lot of bread, I know, but the football's better now than I can ever remember and we've started winning things, which is what it's all about at the end of the day. You can go on about the money players get, but fair play to them. If a player can get twenty, thirty grand a week all I say is lucky bastard! You telling me you wouldn't take it? I only feel sorry for the great players who just missed out – players like Peter Osgood, Dave Webb, Peter Bonetti. They were as good in their day but, like I say, football's changed. Well, club football has, anyway.

The stark reality is that the number of world-class players presently pulling on the Three Lions can be counted on a hand of Jeremy Beadle proportions, something clearly borne out by the fact that only one of our entire Euro 2000 squad is currently rated high enough to make his living by travelling in the opposite direction. Managers and directors point out that English players are valued at too high a price by their clubs, forcing them to go abroad in search of better bargains – an argument I find confusing to say the least, as it is those very same directors who raise such asking-prices in the first place! With players such as Michael Owen, Kevin Phillips, Alan Smith and Joe Cole coming through, I do believe English football is capable of producing top-class players, but it is the squad-players who are struggling to surface, while cheap, previously unheard-of imports flood our clubs and bolt the door shut on our promising youth. These are the players who form the back-bone of any great team, and without them there is no future, so something has to be done in order to give them the chance to shine.

With the England team currently playing the role of jester among the world's finest, the time has come for those who run the game to go back to the drawing-board and start laying out a whole new set of plans for the future. However, the one sure-fire thing we all have to face up to is that there is no quick fix and the solution lies not within the Premier League as it is now but much, much further down the line. To their credit the Football Association have recognised this and have taken hold of the problem by promising to siphon vast amounts of money from the new television deals, directing it towards where it is needed most: at grass-roots level. In order to rebuild our foot-balling stature we all have to except that we need to start by investing in the players of the future, not only with money but also with time and patience.

It is a plan the current World and European champions, France, were forced into implementing themselves less than a decade ago – and just look at how it has paid off for those football fans living just across the Channel. Who knows, if the Football Association can deliver the same kind of funding and commit-ment as was offered by their French counterparts, we may well be sitting back ourselves in a few years time, polishing a trophy or two of our own while bemoaning the state of our domestic league and wondering why all our home-grown talent have packed their bags and decided to play their football across that very same stretch of water!

26

And so, The End is Here; English Football R.I.P!

When England get knocked out of a competition that's usually it as far as I'm concerned, the tournament's over, end of story, goodnight, the end! However, at Euro 2000 all that changed, because this time, as much as it hurts to say it, the team's embarrassing exit brought with it an unprecedented sense of relief. My relief was born out of the fact that I had already suffered enough humiliation and that, after witnessing what the likes of Portugal, Italy, Holland and France were capable of, I personally viewed England's early trip home as a blessing in disguise.

Once England had left the Low Countries behind I viewed the remainder of the tournament with wonder. I was dazzled by the skills of players such as Zidane, Totti and Kluivert, and marvelled at the skill, grace and composure each one displayed in abundance when playing what the rest of the world refers to as 'the beautiful game'. Unfortunately, I still had to suffer the humiliation of seeing every team I chose to lend my support to fall by the wayside, as first Portugal and then Holland dipped out of the contest. And although Turkey's elimination did bring some relief, I have to admit that the sight of seeing France bag yet another pot after coming back from the dead to beat Italy in the final felt like one final kick in the gonads from what had been a long hard tournament. However, as I sat back in awe I also found myself feeling cheated, cheated by those who have allowed English football to stand motionless while the rest of the world pulled on their boots and jogged off to distant playing fields. As I have already stated, I am not naïve enough to think England has some God-given right to be rubbing shoulders with the world's best, but surely in a time when the coffers of our domestic game are spilling over we deserve and should be delivering better.

England were without doubt second rate at Euro 2000, appearing to be nothing more than a poor relation making up the numbers until the big guns got down to the real business of sorting out their own pecking order. The vast number of foreign players currently working within our league set-up has undeniably added to the problems we now face at international level, and so, as fans, we have to ask ourselves what we value most: a strong England team capable of taking on the world's finest, or having the globe's top domestic league ruled by three clubs and the greed they induce, while the rest do their best to keep within touching distance? As a fan of a side outside the top flight, I know where my allegiances lie. To their credit, I believe the Football Association have set the ball rolling as far as this issue is concerned. Their planned investment at both grass-roots and youth levels is the only way forward if England are ever to regain credibility among the world's football elite, but as fans we have to remain patient as the planting of new seeds will undoubtedly take a long time to bear fruit.

As we enter the new century, I can't help but feel that football has transformed itself beyond all recognition as the ideal of genuine sportsmanship gives way to the win-at-all-costs ethos that currently rules. The constant failure by our leading managers to see any decision going any way but their own irritates beyond belief, while their dismissing of any allegation levelled against their own players leaves little room for sympathy should things genuinely turn against them. The present level of cheating among the players is nothing short of a disgrace and yet, at the same time, those players pour scorn on the very man they set out to fool if ever the referee signals a wrong decision. I think all fans truly interested in the sport deserve and should demand better from their so-called 'sporting' heroes. However, if it really is all just about the winning, rather than the sport as some say, then maybe we probably end up getting everything we deserve whenever football's circus comes to town. At times I find it hard to view the modern game as anything other than a circus. Agents often justify the vast amounts of money they bleed from the game by comparing the modern-day footballer to the world's great entertainers and if, like me, you consider much of today's football to be a ninety minute show full of gamesmanship and play acting rather than fair play and sportsmanship, it's not hard to see from where I draw my comparisons. If players and fans live by the sword, they must be prepared to die by it and so stop the constant whinging that is currently rife and take the modern game for what it is. Of course everyone wants to win, but no matter what happens on or off the pitch the players, like all entertainers, get paid, the punters turn out in their thousands and, just like the circus, many of the same old faces come to town year after year.

For the travelling fans Euro 2000 not only brought with it the usual problems such as aggressive policing and one-sided journalism but also the back-stabbing by both the Turks and European football's governing body UEFA, all of which points to this particular side of English football facing an even tougher journey back to the top than those who actually play the game. Just how the Turkish support or the Belgian police managed to wash their hands of any involvement in the violence that occurred during the tournament astounds me to this day. The treatment dished out by the Belgian authorities was nothing short of a disgrace as their officers spilt blood, cracked skulls and ordered deportations at will. I sincerely believe that the level of aggression hammered out towards the English clearly demonstrated a desire to relieve themselves of over fifteen years of hurt following the Heysel disaster, and yet, had they followed the example set by the: Dutch counterparts, we all might well have been celebrating the most trouble-free tournament since Euro 96 rather than cursing the battles of Brussels and Charleroi. There can be no denying that the policing of the English fans plays a major role in what follows as the different methods adopted by the Dutch and Belgium's demonstrated beyond doubt. The fact that the British government jumped to everyone's defence other than their own countrymen shall remain a thorn in the side of many travelling English supporters as they bowed to outside pressure and ducked from international disharmony.

Both the government's and in particular the National Criminal Intelligence Unit's failure to deal with the problem of football violence was once again openly exposed by Euro 2000, but rather than introduce well thought-out legislation to contain the problem, they quickly succumbed to knee-jerk reaction that has not only produced new laws that fly in the face of the notion 'innocent until proven guilty' but are also riddled with loopholes. While the new 'Football Disorder Bill' does contain the long overdue combining of both domestic and international banning orders along with the requirement for known offenders to surrender their passports, it also fails to take effect once you cross the border into Scotland, a loophole that allows the serious hooligan the luxury of starting their trip from either Glasgow or Edinburgh unrestricted.

However, there is one measure within the bill that totally oversteps the mark, as suddenly the fundamental right of every British citizen is laid to rest. The fact that any football fan can now be arrested and detained purely on the 'grounds' that he might cause trouble in the future quite frankly rips the very heart out of our once respected justice system as it lays each and every one of us open to the shocking reality of The Thought Police. As with the Criminal Justice Bill, the government has used football to squeeze through laws of which the vast majority of the public remain blissfully unaware. To me it is quite sickening that the government has used football in this way especially as they claim new laws demanded by the public to protect children from paedophiles and frightened homeowners from burglars are so difficult to implement. What strange times we live in.

For the vast majority Euro 2000 was a trouble-free festival of football. A fact that went largely unrecognised and un-reported by the once respected British press but still remains the very reason why so many thousands go back year after year, championship after championship, and long shall that remain. No matter what others say about this country, I remain fiercely proud of England and of my fellow countrymen. I also retain my passion for English football, its supporters and the England international football team, for it is the only true English football any of us have left . . . Or at least it was!

Unlike most, I refuse to blame Keegan for England's shambolic showing. While many claim the man was tactically naïve, we all have to accept that without quality players even the best-laid plans count for nothing. I don't for one minute believe Kevin Keegan to be a world-class manager, but if the Football Association will insist on sacking better men because of their religious convictions or let them slip through their fingers due to personality clashes then I genuinely believe there was no one more suited to take up the reins at the time of his appointment. For me, Keegan achieved wonders by just getting the team to qualify in the first place, but from then on he was always fighting an uphill battle as his England stars simply found themselves wanting in the face of top-quality opposition. I believe Keegan realised his squad's shortcomings well in advance and did all he could by instilling a sense of self-belief and cameraderie among his players in the hope that it would pull them through when in reality blind hope was clearly never going to be enough. I just can't help thinking it a touch unfor-tunate that some of his squad couldn't return such faith in Keegan once they had under-performed. As ever the Great British press were quickly sharpening the knives and began calling for the England manager's head and, sure enough, they had their moment following that fateful day when England lost to the Germans in the last match ever to be played at Wembley.

Keegan's resignation turned England's international future

on its head and clearly demonstrated that blame lies with those who have for so long let the game slip into the abyss, the Football Association. In their desperate search for a new coach the FA was found wanting, largely due to the exposure of their own failings. The petty rows and ego-driven decisions made from within those walls had not only left English football without any up and coming world-class young coaches, but also continued long enough to cost the nation the people's choice as Keegan's replacement, Terry Venables. Despite calls from fans, players, ex-World Cup winners and the media, many of the invisible faces that rule over the game in this country refused to budge and so English football sold its soul and went in search of a foreign coach.

I have never in all my years felt so ashamed, betrayed and disgusted. How could the Football Association do this to our nation? To me, the England team meant everything and yet in one foul swoop they stole it from my veins, from now on it would never be the same. The whole ethos behind international football is for teams from differing nations and backgrounds to come together and compete against one another. It's as simple as that, no arguing. A team comprising purely of nationals from whatever country they happen to be born into. It isn't league football, a free-for-all, come and grab the money bonanza, this is a representation of the nation you grew up in, but to some even that gives way to the desire to win at all cost . . . Have they no pride?

I honestly feel sicken by the fact that the England team and all those that follow her have been sold off so cheaply. Who the hell do these people think they are? David Davies, an ex-television presenter for Christs sake! What gives him the right to be fucking with our national pride? All I can do now is sit back and wonder whether or not they honestly understand the can of worms they have so eagerly opened up for themselves, for if not, then boy had they better start reaching for the tin hats because as a fan that has followed England abroad on numerous occasions please believe me when I tell you that Mr Davies , Mr Crozier and chums are in for one hell of a rough ride. To many it will not matter a monkey's tit whether England win, lose or draw, for supporting England, as with any other side, is not just about what happens out on the pitch. A foreign boss could bring home the World Cup surrounded by a hundred naked dancing girls doing cartwheels. He could carry the Euro pot head high and even chuck the Holy Grail in for good measure but it simply wouldn't mean a thing due to one minor detail, he ain't English and that is something I don't think many will ever let Davies and pals forget. And you can jot me down as a member of that particular little club right here and now.

However, before I finish may I take the liberty of reminding you of one last thing . . . OK, so it was a disaster, England were shite and the violence opened up all those old wounds once more, but sod it, at least we beat the fucking Germans! All together now:

> 1–0 to the Eng-ger-land,
> 1–0 to the Eng-ger-land,
> 1–0 to the Eng-ger-land,
> 1–0 to the Eng-ger-land,

Capital Punishment

Dougie and Eddy Brimson

London is home to some of British football's most notorious hooligans. However, the history of such infamous 'firms' as the ICF, the Headhunters and the Bushwhackers has never been fully documented . . . until now.

From the authors of the bestselling *Everywhere We Go* and *England, My England* comes a remarkable and frank examination of football violence involving the supporters of clubs from the capital. They explain not only how these groups have gained and maintained their reputations, but also why hooligans from other parts of the country see a trip to London as their biggest challenge, and how the system of public transport opens up opportunities for those who wish to fight. Each of the major clubs is studied to assess why some seem to attract a more violent following than others and to explain how different inter-club and inter-regional rivalries have evolved. *Capital Punishment* is an eye-opening study of a problem that refuses to go away.

Reviews for their previous books:

Everywhere We Go . . . 'probably the best book ever written on football violence' *Daily Mail*

England, My England . . . 'quite simply brilliant!' *Sky Sports Magazine*

NON-FICTION / SPORT   0 7472 5713 2